Codependency, Sexuality, and Depression

by
William E. Thornton, M.D.

T·H·E
PIA
PRESS

19 Prospect Street
Summit, NJ 07901

This book is not intended to replace personal medical care and/or professional supervision; there is no substitute for the experience and information that your doctor or mental health professional can provide. Rather, it is our hope that this book will provide additional information to help people understand the nature of codependency and psychiatric conditions that can evolve.

Proper treatment should always be tailored to the individual. If you read something in this book that seems to conflict with your doctor or mental health professional's instructions, contact him/her. There may be sound reasons for recommending treatment that may differ from the information presented in this book.

If you have any questions about any treatment in this book, please consult your doctor or mental health care professional.

In addition, the names and cases used in this book do not represent actual people, but are composite cases drawn from several sources.

Cover photo by Bert Stern

Contents

DEDICATION

To my patients who constantly teach me,
by sharing their internal worlds.

ACKNOWLEDGMENTS

Most important, I am grateful to my wife, Duffy and entire family for their encouragement, support and tolerance. Also, I thank Dan Montopoli, Rochelle Ratner and Ron Schaumberg for their talents.

About the Author

William E. Thornton, MD, received his M.D. from Vanderbilt University, following which he studied Internal Medicine at the University of Wisconsin, and Psychiatry at the Johns Hopkins University. Dr. Thornton was the author of many scientific publications and a national lecturer for physicians while he was a full-time faculty member at the Universities of Chicago, Illinois, South Carolina, and Johns Hopkins. Most recently he was Clinical Professor of Psychiatry and Associate Professor of Family Practice at the University of Nevada. Dr. Thornton has been a member of many professional organizations including the American Society of Physician Analysts and the Johns Hopkins Medical and Surgical Society. He is a fellow in the Academy of Psychosomatic Medicine and a founding member of the American Academy of Psychiatrists in Alcoholism and Addiction. Currently Dr. Thornton is the Medical Director of the Slidell Center for Psychotherapy and the NorthShore Psychiatric Hospital.

1

■————————————————■

Codependency:
The Consumer's Diagnosis

A few years ago a woman—I'll call her Sheryl*—came to see me.

"Why can't I be married and happy? Everything seems to be falling apart around me."

Sheryl was a neat, attractive woman in her mid-thirties. I pressed for details. "I try to be the best wife and mother I can," Sheryl said. "I give my husband Bob all the freedom he asks for. I pretty much raise the kids by myself, I take care of the house and the bills. But somehow it doesn't seem to be enough. He still seems angry with me all the time. Sometimes I think he hates me. What's wrong with me?"

During this session and those that followed, I learned more of the details of Sheryl's life. This was actually her second marriage. Her first had been to a man named Steve, with whom she had two children. She described Steve as a "good father but a poor provider." Not only did Sheryl, a real estate broker, supply most of the family income, she was also more intelligent and better educated than Steve. Sheryl found that sex with Steve soon became a very unfulfilling experience, one that both of them did their best to avoid. After their divorce she took custody of the children. Steve rarely made his child support payments. Sheryl's mother, who lived only a few blocks away, usually looked after the kids; often she would even stay for dinner and sleep over.

---

*All patient names and identifying characteristics have been changed to protect privacy.

Between marriages Sheryl had many sexual contacts, and she became "proud" that she could be sexually aggressive with men. She dyed her hair, worked out at the gym five times a week, and dressed "to show off my body."

Eight years ago she married Bob, whom she described as "handsome, a real corporate climber, and very aggressive sexually." While she said their sex life was very passionate, Bob tended to be highly critical of her mothering abilities and her social skills. One year he refused to take her to his office Christmas party, saying, "You'll just embarrass me by saying something stupid, like you always do."

The worst moments came during those arguments when Bob would dredge up Sheryl's sexual past, which usually happened after he'd had too much to drink. He would call her a "slut" and a "whore." And on a few occasions he would hit her—or, as he put it, "try to slap some sense into you." Often his words and actions infuriated her. She was becoming frightened of a rage within herself that she hadn't known existed. "But what bothers me most," said Sheryl, "is that *I'm* always the one who apologizes afterward. He always forgives me and is very sweet; nine times out of ten we end an argument by making love. But I wake up in the morning feeling even worse than I did before."

Gradually Bob's drinking became even more of a problem. "I could deal with the booze," Sheryl said. "It was when I found out he was seeing other women—and had been practically since the day we were married—that I began thinking this has got to stop."

One day, watching television, she caught one of those ubiquitous talk shows. The theme of the show was: "Addicted to Love—With the Wrong Men!" As Sheryl put it, the show struck a chord somewhere deep inside her. For the first time she heard about the concept of *codependency*.

The show also mentioned a few books available on the subject, so she bought everything the bookstore had. One of the books mentioned a toll-free number to call for further help and information. By calling that number Sheryl found out about a codependency self-help group in her area. She joined and attended meetings regularly.

During those sessions, Sheryl discovered that, like all people, she wanted her relationships to provide her with respect, security, and happiness. Yet for some reason she had become trapped in a degrading, sadomasochistic pattern, a pattern that repeated itself in cycles—first with Steve, then with Bob. She was unable to break that cycle, to make the decisions that would free her from her pattern and would help her realize that she was a person to be valued, not abused.

For the first time, Sheryl felt better. She continued to read self-help books and attended the self-help meetings. Her husband ridiculed her—"You actually believe that trash?" he would sneer. But Sheryl knew she was onto something. She felt better about herself, although she still suffered from feelings of inferiority. Worse, though, was that despite her burgeoning self-awareness, her relationship with Bob wasn't getting any better.

Then: catastrophe. Sheryl's mother with whom she had been very close, died after a prolonged and painful illness. Sheryl handled all the arrangements herself and still managed to run the household and continue working. Despite her nearly superhuman efforts, Bob continued to torment her with his sarcastic remarks, disparaging her handling of the situation. He also stayed out several nights each week; Sheryl suspected—and her suspicions were later confirmed—that he was turning up the heat in his extramarital affairs.

It was too much. Sheryl felt like a complete failure. "Look at me, I can't even leave Bob, I can't even follow the advice in these books. What's wrong with me? I feel so empty." She began to think about suicide.

But there was a spark in Sheryl, a force that wouldn't let her give up. Sheryl knew she had to do something drastic to turn her life around. Finally she came to NorthShore Psychiatric Hospital.

That's when I first met her.

The fact that Sheryl's first exposure to the idea of codependency came from a TV talk show suggests once again that the lay public can often be ahead of the experts. In essence, the public had emphasized the existence of a problem long before it entered the medical textbooks. Sheryl was the first patient—but not the last—to enter my office convinced that she was a codependent.

One magazine article claimed that there are perhaps 40 million codependent people in the country today. I realized there were probably a lot of other people out there who had never heard of codependency but were still trying to figure out what had gone wrong with their lives and their relationships.

These were the people who thought that when they grew up, became adults, and got married and raised families or landed the job of their dreams, they were supposed to be Happy with a capital H. "But why," they ask themselves, just as Sheryl had asked me, *why don't I feel good about myself?*"

These people were beginning to band together, doing all they could to help each other in self-help programs based on the principles of Alcoholics Anonymous. However, I suspected this wasn't enough. Sure, there are many parallels between being chemically dependent and being codependent, but I suspected that the solutions to codependency might not be as simple as following the "Twelve-Step" plans derived from Alanon or Alcoholics Anonymous. Similarly, meditating or reading a spiritual book might make people feel better for a brief time, but that wasn't going to make their problems disappear. After you close the book, after the meditation session is over, you are still alone with yourself—a "self" that may lack any sense of self-esteem or self-respect.

Whenever a "fad illness" makes headlines or becomes a subject for TV talk shows, there is a danger that many people might be prematurely, casually—even wrongly—labeled as having that condition. Just diagnosing "codependency" as a problem is meaningless unless we know how to *treat* that condition. But which treatments work? Which strategies do nothing more than help people get through a crisis temporarily, and which ones offer more permanent solutions? Does treatment pose any risk of harm? Are there lasting—and dangerous—side effects? We had to find out.

To answer these and other questions, we needed to learn more about the pathways by which people developed codependent problems. I felt it was time for mental health professionals to step in and find out more about what was going on.

THE STORY SO FAR

Over the last two decades our understanding of alcoholism and drug addiction has grown enormously. For one thing, study after study has shown that chemical dependencies often run in families. We also learned how chemical dependency affects not just the addicts themselves, but their entire families. Programs such as Alanon, aimed at families of alcoholics, began working side by side with AA. But still, it was the addicted person who continued to receive the most attention. Those few programs that involved other family members focused, not on their own needs, but on how to help the chemically dependent person recover.

Finally the families themselves stepped in and said: "Wait a minute, there's something wrong with this picture. We're suffering, too. We've got problems just as big as those of our addicted fathers, or mothers, or husbands, or wives, or children. It's time for someone to give *us* a little of that attention, and we shouldn't have to slit our wrists or take antidepressants in order to draw the focus in our direction."

But families still didn't get much response from the psychologists and social workers, nor were there enough support groups. So they took matters into their own hands. They began by giving their problem a name. For lack of a better word, they called themselves *co*dependents. Health-care consumers had invented their own diagnosis.

The publicity that the subject of codependency received was helpful—at least in one respect. Sheryl, remember, first sought help because of a TV program. Books have been an aid to people, too. Authors, some of whom are themselves recovering codependents, turned out best-sellers that were instrumental in drawing the public's attention to this problem, which is every bit as complex and enormous as all the addictions put together. Five years ago there was almost no literature available on codependency. Walk into any large bookstore today, and you'll probably see a dozen books on codependency alone, along with related books on the children of alcoholics or women who can't stop loving the wrong men.

Is this a good thing? Somewhat. Many of these books are great at stating that a problem called codependency exists, and that it is a real condition whose victims need help. Where the books fail, though, is in their understanding of the *origins* of codependency and of the in-depth steps we must take to help codependent people.

PAIN WITHOUT A NAME

I had been mulling over the problem of how codependency develops when I went to have dinner with my friends Dave and Ellen. They had just returned from a tour of southern Spain. "When we were in Granada," Ellen told me, "the bus passed a wedding party just as they were leaving the church. The bride and groom got into their car, and those of us sitting on the right side could see she was crying. The tour guide commented, 'The bride has every right to cry—she's making a lifetime decision. Spain is a Catholic country, and there's no such thing as divorce here.'" Ellen knitted her brow. "Doesn't that make you shudder?"

Yes, it did make me shudder—but not for the reason Ellen thought. Quite the opposite: My shudder came from my sudden awareness of how Americans have come to take the concept of divorce so lightly. People here don't think of themselves as married for life anymore. Our marriages are "trial" marriages; we don't take our relationships as seriously as our ancestors did. A recent editorial in *The New York Times*, satirizing the concept of the "prenuptial agreement," quipped: "Honey, here's the deal. I swear to cherish you till death do us part. Or at least until the marriage is no longer working out." I wonder how their yet unborn children would feel about such an attitude.

Over the last 30 years the divorce rate in America and the number of children who abruptly lose a parent as a result has risen almost every year. Sometimes it seems as if the "nuclear family"—two parents, their kids, available grandparents—is becoming extinct. Many children today have never met their natural father—or their mother, for that matter.

Families need money to survive. Often this means the mother is forced to work out of financial necessity. With both parents holding jobs, there can be a lot of strain on the family. The parents are gone most of the day; the care of their children is left to strangers. Women have fought hard to win the right of maternity leave, but even with those companies that grant it, the leave may be for only three to six months—if that. Ironically, then, families sometimes dissolve because the parents were trying their hardest to keep it intact, at least financially.

On the other hand, the mother who *does* take a few years off work after a child is born might well find herself bored by staying home all day. In such cases the family is endangered because the mother feels unsatisfied and unfulfilled.

In other cases the young mother never leaves the work force at all. She's rushing home to pick up the baby before the day-care center closes, trying to stop at the supermarket with an unhappy, fidgety child in the cart, then cook dinner. No wonder she questions the meaningfulness of her marriage.

Whatever the variations on this plot, such women often wake up one morning and realize: *I'm in an unhappy, failing relationship.*

The saga of relationship failure has been a familiar one in American over the past thirty years. Only recently, however, have we been able to give a name to those who are unable to sustain a commitment to their sexual partner. The name helps quite a bit. Codependent people no longer have to suffer in silence; they no longer have to think they're going crazy. They know they're suffering from a very real problem. It might not be in their doctor's diagnostic textbook, but it's a real problem nonetheless. They know that alcoholics can get help at hundreds of treatment centers around the country. They're beginning to realize that there's help available for them, too.

The typical patient will come to me for help after having read the latest book on codependency. These books tend to agree that the adult codependent's problem begins in childhood. Usually, they'll blame the problem on an unloving family that could not function well because of problems with abuse, job failure, or simple low self-esteem. This is a tremendous oversimplification. True, such factors can contribute to adult relationship failures, but as I'll explain in subsequent chapters, the actual origins lie elsewhere.

Not long ago a patient of mine named Jill came in brandishing some photocopied pages from a book about adult children of alcoholics. The passage that excited Jill explained how many such people were forced to assume the role of caretaker for their parents. The author describes how, as children, they had to rush home from school to take care of their brothers and sisters, or make sure Momma hadn't passed out drunk again and whacked her head on the coffee table. The author points out that these children want nothing more than to flee from this strange life, yet are always compelled to return home as soon as possible.

As a consequence, such children never have many friends. They never really learn how friendships work, or have much faith in their abilities to share with others. The authors of the popular books on codependency contend that such children grow up into adults who look for mates who will permit them to continue in this caretaking role, it's the only way they know to relate to people. When the mate finally becomes too much to handle, or if the marriage becomes too depressing, they pull themselves out of it. Then they often repeat the identical pattern with another mate.

"What do you think?" my patients ask when they share these book excerpts with me. I explain that, after twenty-five years of treating dependent people, I see things differently. Codependent people don't simply look for mates who demand a high degree of caretaking just because that's the only role they've ever known. They do so because they are *angry*—deep-down, gut-rotting, mind-blackening angry. The sad part is that these people have suppressed that anger for many years; they have buried it so deep they can't recognize it anymore.

But the anger eventually emerges in disguised form. In this case, the codependent person looks for a mate who requires a high level of "caretaking"—and yes, superficially at least, this appears to be a replay of life with an alcoholic parent. But, in its extreme form, taking care of someone means *controlling* that person. The caretaker gets to decide what the mate does that is right or wrong, good or bad. Left unchecked, the caretaker eventually takes possession of the other person. The unconscious goal of possession—at least in a codependent relationship—is to destroy.

From what my patients tell me, most of the books on codependency point out—correctly, in my view—that the relationship we experienced with the person who cared for us during most of our childhood (usually the mother) will determine how we relate to people for the rest of our lives. It will determine how we relate to our own children and how they, in turn, will function as lovers and parents. Unless, of course, we step in and do something to break the pattern. The basic theme of most of the codependency literature is: If the relationship isn't offering what you want, then you've got to get out of it. *You owe it to yourself to protect yourself.*

For example, children from difficult families, accustomed to ambivalent feelings toward their parents, feel that they cannot just desert them after they strike out to begin families of their own. Often, in a woman's case, her relationship to her parents takes priority over what she, as a wife, can offer her husband. She might get a phone call and rush out of the house, leaving her husband and kids to fend for themselves, because Daddy's drunk again and she has to get over there to cook for him and pour him into bed. (The attachment between parent and adult child can be especially strong in families where there was a problem of incest.) Clearly, this woman needs to learn to protect herself.

So far so good. But at this point the self-help books generally fail to show the reader what the next step is. They tell people that they have to protect themselves—fine. But then the writers admit that many people suffering from codependency don't have a strong sense of who they are. Here's my question: How can you protect yourself if you don't know who "yourself" is?

Some popular authors on codependency come closer to recognizing this problem than others. One patient showed me a passage from a book by Melody Beattie, who wrote: "Some people are fortunate enough to emerge into adulthood knowing who they are, and what their rights are and aren't. They don't trespass on other people's territory, and they don't allow others to invade theirs. They have healthy boundaries and a solid sense of self. Unfortunately, many of us emerged into adulthood with damaged, scarred, or nonexistent boundaries."

But, the codependent asks, how can I establish those boundaries and build up my sense of self? How can I repair a lifetime of damage and make my life worth living again? Unfortunately, the books don't have much to offer by way of answering such crucial questions, and positive self-affirmations are usually short-lived.

Which is why people who are codependent—the lucky ones, anyway—realize they must turn to professional help.

"TELL ME HOW TO MAKE THIS RELATIONSHIP WORK!"

From my quarter-century of work in this field, I know that the study of codependency means learning how relationships *fail* as well as how they *form*. I've also realized that a good relationship allows partners to balance their dependence—sharing their lives with loved ones—with their need for independence. To form good relationships, people must admit their need to be both dependent and independent and *to exert these needs aggressively*. These two critical needs—dependence and independence—can be seen either as assets or liabilities; which they are in a given relationship depends upon the partners involved.

That's where, as adults, we have a choice. That's where therapy can help restore the balance.

Today we know more about codependents like Sheryl. We have a good idea of what's going to happen when a woman with a poor sense of herself—an "underdeveloped personality" —marries a man who degrades her. We know more about why the couple down the street, who for six years looked like they had the perfect marriage, are suddenly divorcing. And we're learning why women are the ones who tend to blame themselves.

SHERYL'S STORY, CONTINUED

Over the weeks that followed her initial visit, Sheryl made tremendous progress in therapy. The first breakthrough came when she realized that her relationships hadn't *failed;* they had been *destroyed.* Even more important was her dawning awareness that *she herself had participated actively in their destruction.*

In our subsequent sessions we focused on the issue of why she helped destroy the thing she most valued. Sheryl discovered that she possessed enormous reservoirs of hatred and rage, emotions that she had always denied. She realized that she had tried to release some of these emotions through her sexual wantonness following her divorce. Although she claimed she had no trouble achieving orgasm, she eventually confessed that she could only climax if *she* controlled the pace and intensity of foreplay, and that the physical intimacy of intercourse provided her with little pleasure.

Sheryl saw that both of her marriages were to men whom she could never respect. In choosing these "relationship losers," she had provided herself with convenient outlets for the rage and hate she had denied for so long. As she put it, "When I picked these guys, I was guaranteeing myself that I would have someone around to blame for my misery."

In our conversations, Sheryl recalled having trouble forming her own identity. "Mom seemed so lonely and depressed—I felt that she needed me to make her happy," she remembered. "Daddy was never home. I brought mother gifts to make her happy. I stayed home with her." Separating from the family was particularly traumatic, with anxiety that persisted for years. After each marriage Sheryl insisted that they live near her mother—"She's sick, she needs to have me around," she told her husbands. The big breakthrough in her therapy occurred when Sheryl realized that her failure to establish satisfying relationships as an adult were replays of the problems she had had as a child in her relationship with her first love: her mother.

Sheryl worked through her separation fears *with* me in long-term therapy. Then the successful process of separating *from* me produced her long-sought sense of identity. I saw Sheryl again not long ago; she dropped by the hospital to say hello and let me know how she was doing. She looks terrific. She divorced Bob and is now seeing a "wonderful man, someone who understands what I've been through and loves me in spite of it." Something tells me that this relationship might last.

IS DEPENDENCY "BAD"?

All of us long for lasting, fulfilling relationships. At best, being involved with another person means being mutually dependent. After all, if we don't depend on the others to supply us with with love, encouragement, or support, of what use is the relationship in the first place? My point is that "dependency" in and of itself is not necessarily a bad thing.

The trouble arises when people use relationships as a *substitute* for developing a strong self-identity. Instead of recognizing their own deep feelings, they suppress them. Then they seek relationships in which they can exploit the other person as their main means of releasing these feelings. Sheryl, for example, felt a deep-seated loathing for her sexual promiscuousness. Each meaningless sexual encounter was another failed effort to prove to herself that she was aggressive and independent, when in fact, and she somehow knew it—it revealed her fears of intimacy and her lonely isolation. When she remarried, she chose a man whom she knew to be a "womanizer" and whom she came to detest. She used Bob as her personal whipping boy, an outlet for her feelings of self-disgust and fears of closeness.

As I said, dependency is not necessarily bad. *Codependency,* however, is. Codependency—which means simply "dependence together" refers to the failure of a dependent relationship due to our denying our aggressiveness and hostilities, projecting them onto our partner, then feeling depressed and victimized. *One's* unhappiness is always the *other's* fault. Sadly, codependent relationships become the arena for hostility, control, possessiveness, and mutual destruction. Those who are codependent may see themselves as nothing more than empty vessels; they rely on other people to fill them with love, with security. Of course, relationships stand a much better chance of succeeding if neither person sees himself or herself as "empty," but as having certain qualities and assets that complement the other's. Happiness requires that the need to give love is at least equal to the need to get it.

As I'll demonstrate throughout this book, the problem of codependency has its roots in childhood personality development. Indeed, people can be set on the path of codependency from the moment they are born. But if our primal need to feel loved by our parents has been fulfilled, and if our parents accept and understand that our struggle to separate from them is part of the natural order of things and therefore a development to be welcomed, then we will be prepared as adults to seek out and establish rewarding dependent relationships. If not, problems arise; problems that are intricately interwoven with our sexuality and mental well-being.

As a doctor I am convinced that codependency can be treated. *You can break the destructive patterns of the past and help yourself by understanding the roots of your codependency.* That's why I wrote this book.

However, I must warn you: *Some of my thoughts about codependency may surprise you.* But I also believe that they can help you.

Over the past two years, my colleagues and I have worked with hundreds of patients in our program at NorthShore Psychiatric Hospital, outside of New Orleans. People often come to us because a friend of theirs went through our program and they saw the changes in that person. Or they come to us because they were looking through the self-help section at the local bookstore and wound up talking to someone who suggested they call us. The NorthShore treatment program began because the public demanded it. As health-care consumers, people first discovered the self-diagnosis of codependency, then turned to those of us in the field of medicine and demanded that we find a way of treating the condition.

We don't have all the answers yet. But this book is a first step in sharing with you, the public, some of our groundbreaking observations about relationships that work and relationships that don't work.

For example, we discovered that *codependency arises from*

problems that affect the way an individual's personality develops.

Don't jump to conclusions. We're not saying that codependency is "all your fault." Codependency is the result of patterns in relationships, patterns that began to affect you even before you were born and that continued to have an impact as you grew through the stages of life. Seen in this way, however, codependency is a problem that can only be resolved by recognizing those patterns and working hard to alter them. That, in turn, will only happen if you agree to take a much closer—and deeper—look at yourself than the popular books on codependency recommend.

Although some of the thoughts in this book might seem complex, our message is basically simple: *You don't have to keep repeating the same codependency patterns over and over.* You don't have to settle for misery and pain from relationships, even in the relationship you currently find so troubling.

I'm not making any promises, but I *am* offering realistic hope. In this book I will ask you to make a commitment to being interested in yourself: how your personality has developed and how this affects your relationships. That commitment may demand more of you than other books on this subject do, but rest assured: In the end, the results will be much more rewarding—and enduring.

2

A Natural History of Dependency

Every creature on earth begins life completely dependent on others of the species for survival. But in the animal world, ties to the parents are quickly broken.

Look at the eagle, for example. When Mother Eagle thinks her offspring are ready to fly, she carries them in the air and drops them. On the off chance they're not prepared, she'll catch them and try again later. But once the baby eagle finds himself flying alone, he knows instinctively that the time has come for him to take care of himself. He doesn't stop in midair and begin questioning who he is. He knows he's this little bird up there with his wings spread, sailing along on an updraft. He knows, too, he has to stay on the lookout for food; if he doesn't find it there's nobody who's going to feed him. In the course of nature, his mother has nurtured him and then abandoned him; now he has to take care of himself.

Humans are the only species who must be cared for by the parents for many years. Most children are dependent on other people, at least through puberty. That's about 15 or 20 percent of a person's life!

Many parents try to possess the child long after that period. Even as adults, with children of our own, we humans are still expected to love, honor, and respect our parents.

It's worth spending time here discovering how the nature of our dependency changes over the course of infancy and childhood. In doing so we'll discover how and where things might inadvertently "go wrong"—and how such problems lead to the problems of codependency.

MADONNA AND CHILD

Before birth, we are literally fused with our mothers' bodies. Experts have written volumes on so-called "birth trauma," the shocks that occurs when babies suddenly find themselves "separate." But in reality, as newborns we don't experience ourselves as separate—we see everything in the world as part of ourselves. The period of fusion with the mother's body, and the memory of that fusion, is imprinted forever in our minds. We never escape our biological need to be loved. It is this need which, as we go through life, gives rise to all our feelings of love, desire, longing, and hope.

As newborns, our muscles have no ability to do work—no "tone" that enables us to differentiate our limbs. We will thus unconsciously mold our bodies to fit snugly against the mother's. We make no distinction between the breast that provides our food and the mouth we use to receive that food. Placed in a crib, we can't roll over by ourselves, but if Mother comes and changes our position to make us more comfortable, we experience that comfort as emanating from ourselves. Within the first few weeks we begin to distinguish pain from pleasure—hunger as distinct from food—but we have no conception that the hunger comes from inside ourselves while food is provided by the outside world.

On a subconscious level, however, even as infants we are aware of our dependence. We realize we cannot soothe our own hunger, so we begin to cry until we are fed. As the British psychoanalyst Joan Riviere has described the process: "[The infant] automatically explodes, as it were, with hate and aggressive craving. If he feels emptiness and loneliness, an automatic reaction sets in, which may soon become uncontrollable and overwhelming, an aggressive rage which brings pain and explosive, burning, suffocating, choking bodily sensations; and these in turn cause further feelings of lack, pain, and apprehension."

These two basic drives—*dependency* (affiliation, or the need for union) and *aggression* (destruction, or the need to discharge built-up energy)—are unavoidable elements of the human condition. Were it not for our need to protect ourselves from our own anger by turning it outward, projecting it onto the world, we might not be as quick to differentiate between ourselves and others. As infants we see ourselves as omnipotent and totally "good"; anything "bad" comes from outside ourselves.

BABY LOOK, BABY SEE

At approximately five months, while Mother holds us, we strain backward to get a better look at her. We poke a finger at her nose or eyes as we explore her face. At this age, our ability to differentiate is still incomplete. As far as an infant knows, the parts of the body are interchangeable, and objects can replace people. A pacifier or the nipple on a bottle can thus substitute for the nipple on the mother's breast. As infants we experience pleasure in putting such things into our mouths, and will try to recreate the same pleasure by putting a toy or our fingers into our mouth. Anything that gives pleasure is not just *associated* with the mother; to the primitive, infantile mind it *becomes* the mother.

If this total fusion with the mother continued after birth— if the mother's body could always satisfy all our needs—we would never discover the need to assert ourselves. It is the experience of frustration that prompts us to begin to fend for ourselves. We must discover an object in the world that will satisfy us until the mother becomes available. As our needs grow we must discover a wider number of substitute objects. The French psychoanalyst Janine Chasseguet-Smirgel observes, "It is from having to delay satisfaction that phantasy life, the elaboration of desire, language, etc. is born."

An infant's fantasy life is much more complex than most people realize, and it contains both love and hate. As long as a baby's needs are satisfied by the breast, the baby retains pleasurable memories of it; when he is frustrated by the breast's absence, or the lack of milk, he fantasizes attacking the breast, eating it up, devouring it, destroying it (and his mother as well). To realize how true this is, we need merely consider how early the infant will begin to bite the mother's breast. A mother often dismisses this biting, saying, "He doesn't know how strong he is," but in a sense it represents an attack by the frustrated infant.

"MINE!"

As children, our awareness of the outside world gradually grows. We begin to experience Mother not just as a "breast" but as a whole person. Because we now recognize her love, we no longer experience the earlier fantasies of persecution. A new emotion enters our world: *guilt*. Anger and frustration are still pent up inside, but we transform much of that energy into the worry that Mother is in danger. At night, we might ask to sleep with Mother's blouse or sweater, to help keep the image of Mother closer when we feel alone, and also to reassure ourselves that we haven't harmed her somehow.

The more children's physical abilities increase, the more they notice and respond to the outside world. From about 8 to 16 months of age (the time when locomotion is discovered), children go through the "practicing" phase of development— they literally *practice* their ability to function on their own. At this stage our sense of ourselves remains omnipotent, but now it is fragile and continually in need of Mother's reassurance. At first, a child might play on the floor at Mother's feet, perhaps looking up every few minutes to make certain she's there. If indeed she *is* there, and if there have been no major traumatic incidents up to now, the child will begin to play farther away—on the other side of the room, perhaps. Toys, strangers, and other objects from the outside world will attract attention.

Usually children claim one special toy, or object. A popular example of this behavior is in the "Peanuts" comic strip, where Linus refuses to give up his blanket. Children lay claim to such objects in the same way that, as infants, they claim their mothers. Like the blanket or the teddy bear, this newfound possession has a warmth all its own. Now, however, children understand that this warmth comes from *outside* themselves. The toy is separate, but they *control* it—they hug it against themselves; it doesn't move closer on its own. They will cuddle this toy, and sometimes in moments of frustration they might throw it against a wall.

It's important that this special toy withstand both love and hate for as long as the child needs to hang onto it. The child will not forget the old toy, but he will not miss it, either. It was a substitute for his mother, but he knows it never replaced her.

At this stage children experience a love affair with the world around them. They are excited by everything they see, but do not realize that going out into this world means leaving Mother behind. They delight in saying "bye-bye" to her and then running off, because they are confident Mother will come and swoop them up in her arms. That's what makes exploring so much fun.

BEING SEPARATE

During the next stage, roughly between 16 months and two years, children experience themselves as separate and alone. Instead of seeing their mothers as an object whose function is to help them play a game, they realize *she might choose* not to play. Sometimes mother not only refuses to play, but she sometimes goes away, leaving them with other people. Children become lonely, frightened, and anxious. They express these emotions through their *aggressive tendencies*—not just in fantasy but in reality as well.

At this stage children are ambivalent, experiencing dependency and aggression simultaneously. On the one hand, they want to be close to Mother. They are continually checking to see where she is, bringing her presents, running *toward* her instead of away from her. On the other hand, they want to be able to move freely about on their own. They learn to say "no!"; they don't want to be touched; they run away without expecting to be swooped up again in her arms; they may throw temper tantrums either when she comes after them or when she abandons them.

When Mother is around, they might play nicely. They retain a good image of her in their minds, an image that unites with their own image of themselves as "good." But when Mother leaves, they might bang their toys on the floor—they are expressing a fantasy in which they attack her and punish her for going away. When Mother returns they might "rescue" the toy, thereby "rescuing" Mother (and their feelings about her). In other words, the child responds to things and events in the "real" world by dividing them into two categories: external presences and internal representations.

At this stage children are more conscious of their fantasies and what they mean. Fantasies allow children to "harm" the "bad" mother, but they also allow children to repair any damage. This ability to appease or repair helps transform the child's feelings of guilt into feelings of hopefulness. As the eminent child psychoanalyst Melanie Klein has pointed out, during this stage, "making reparation—which is such an essential part of the ability to love—widens in scope, and the child's ability to accept love and, by various means, to take into himself goodness from the outer world steadily increases. This satisfactory balance between 'give' and 'take' is the primary condition for further happiness."

All children must discover their own ways of dealing with their dawning realization that they are separate beings. But here's one of the most important things we've learned in our work with codependent patients: *Whatever a child's initial reaction to separation, that reaction will determine how he reacts to the failure of all his future relationships.* In our experience most of the people who call the various "hotlines" for help with problems are people who have never satisfactorily recovered from the ambivalence they experienced as a result of their first separation and who are experiencing relationship failures in the present.

At this stage, then, children must learn to resolve the conflict between their fears of losing Mother and their excitement at setting off on their own to explore the environment. If it isn't resolved, those conflicts will reappear *continually* in adulthood, and often will lead to codependency problems.

TRUST, PRIDE, AND UNDERSTANDING

As growing children adapt to the world around them, their trust in it increases. They learn how to do "reality checks," testing their fantasies against the world around them. When small children are hungry, they might express their feelings in fantasy form by angrily banging a toy against the floor. Through trial and error, they learn that acting out this fantasy doesn't do anything to ease their hunger. They might then try various other fantasies, until they learn that fantasizing about food, then actually asking for food, works to produce the desired result.

By age three, most children have learned to cope well with their identities as separate beings. They have integrated the "bad" mother with the "good" mother, love with hate. Their thoughts, more or less conscious, run something like this: "Mother isn't around at this moment to feed me or play a game with me. But I remember other good things about her, and I know I don't have to destroy Mother just to make me feel good about myself." Children get angry, but at the same time they can balance that anger with their knowledge that Mother will return, that she's not going to stay away forever. They know too that, even if they do express anger, it won't destroy Mother or her love. Children at this stage can now redirect the energy that formerly fueled their angry fantasies into rebuilding their self-esteem.

MOTHERS LETTING GO

From the moment children recognize their mother as a whole person—not merely a "breast" or a "face"—they begin to regret their anger at their mother's absence. At the same time, they fear for her safety from the destructiveness of their rage. These two opposing emotions must be confronted and reconciled; if not, the child's future development will be rocky, at best. For most children, this reconciliation depends on the mother's loving and responsive guidance. Unfortunately, not all mothers have the requisite skill, sensitivity, or mental health to help their children at this crucial juncture.

To illustrate, let me tell you about Penny. She was one of four children. When Penny was three years old, her mother, who had been bedridden for six months, died. Penny was then totally dependent upon other family members, neighbors, and hired help—just at that stage of development when she needed her mother most. She experienced extreme feelings of abandonment. The resulting fear of being abandoned would affect all of her future relationships.

Now grown, Penny is the mother of a toddler, Amy. As she told me, "I love my child more than I ever thought it possible to love anyone." For Penny, the period just after Amy was born—when Penny was the only person who could soothe or feed her—was the happiest time in her life.

But Penny has some insight into her problem. As she remarked, "I know how important it is for Amy to learn to care for herself. But I love her so much that sometimes I'm afraid to let her out of my sight, even for a moment. So when Amy wants to run across the room, I grit my teeth and pretend to look the other way. I know it's ridiculous, but a part of me is hoping Amy will stumble, so that I can step in and play the 'soothing mother' again." Penny says she watches as other mothers at the playground cheer their children on, encouraging them to run and experience the new things around them. "But I just don't have it in me to do that with Amy."

Penny might not realize it, but she's sending powerful—and dangerous—signals to her child. Even at three, Amy doesn't play with other children well. She'd rather play at her mother's feet, or throw a ball back and forth to her mother (who always throws it back right where Amy's standing). When she *does* break free and run off, it's obvious she doesn't feel too sure of herself. Besides, Amy seems to sense that it hurts Mommy's feelings when she plays with other children. Often in the past, if Amy has played with a friend all day, Mommy will say she's "too tired" to read a story that night. Or, if she does read the story, she won't do all the funny voices or make all the animal growls Amy loves.

Now, as a consequence, when Amy tries to play with other children she finds it hard to remember what she's supposed to do. She's afraid to go on the slide if Mommy's not there to catch her at the bottom. If she sees Mommy talking to someone, she'll come over to where Mommy is sitting and start to dance in front of her. She'll go into a tantrum if Mommy doesn't interrupt her conversation to applaud her. Thus, instead of having fantasies that move closer and closer to reality, Amy's fantasies absorb her in an unrealistic world with unrealistic expectations; at times she doesn't seem to know the difference between what's real and what's not.

You might not know Amy, but you probably know children like her. They're the ones who never seem to adjust in the Head Start programs or nursery schools. They come home tired and frustrated. The mother might try to unbutton their coat, and they run away screaming. The children, of course, don't understand their own rage; it's therefore up to the mother to interpret the signals properly. They have to sense when to leave the children alone and when to offer more assistance—and that's a very hard requirement to meet.

Often mothers in such circumstances throw up their hands in disgust. They think, Oh, give her another ten minutes, she'll stop crying anyway; she'll simply tire herself out. And often that's precisely what happens. The children cry themselves to sleep, or suppress their tears—*but the problem hasn't gone away*. Other insecure mothers might offer children cookies and milk "as soon as you stop crying." Instead of confronting the angry feelings directly, they confuse the child by trying to translate those feelings into something else—hunger, for example.

But such solutions are only temporary at best. The mother's actions may tire the child out, or they may appease the tears; however, they won't help the child learn how to function when Mommy isn't around. These temporary solutions don't help children retain the memory of the "good mother" or to reconcile the good and bad images of the mother. They don't reinforce the child's instincts and observations. Finally, they don't help children develop a unified sense of themselves. Before children can achieve separation, they need to feel confident that they can express anger without "hurting" Mother. They also have to learn that if Mother does leave, there are other people to turn to. *In order for children to grow into healthy adults, there must be at least one other consistent person in their lives on whom they can rely. That person has to be strong enough to offer whatever assurances children aren't getting from their mothers.*

LAURA'S STORY

Whenever I hear people talking about being afraid of their mothers, Laura is the first person I think of.

I met Laura when I was teaching at the University of Chicago. When Laura was two, her mother had a miscarriage and it devastated her. She was in the hospital for two months, close to death. When she came home, Laura's presence only reminded her of her lost baby and her illness. From that time on the mother never paid much attention to Laura, never gave her much love. Laura remembers that every few months during her childhood, her mother would wake up screaming in the middle of the night. Finally the mother was taken to a psychiatric hospital.

Everyone I tell this story to anticipates the ending; they always say something like, "Poor Laura, she must have turned out feeling very empty and devastated." Except that isn't the case. Laura wasn't a patient; she was one of my co-workers. Today Laura is happily married, with two healthy children of her own. After her children started school, Laura went back to college and earned a degree in social work. I hold her up as an example of one of the stronger women I've known.

Despite her childhood trauma, Laura managed to develop a good self-image, form a good marriage, raise a family, and further her own career. How did she manage, when so many other people with mothers who weren't half as bad as hers wind up, as the song puts it, "Looking for Love in All the Wrong Places?" As far as I'm concerned, the difference was Laura's father.

As Laura told it, "Daddy was very strong, a respected businessman and a real committed father. He was able to sit me down and explain in a helpful and loving way how the real world worked. He would say, "I know you heard Mommy crying last night, and I know you're frightened. Now, I realize no matter what I say you're still going to be a little scared. Just remember, though, whenever you're frightened you can always come to me." Through such loving reassurances he gave Laura a sense of stability, and he continued to be a powerful figure throughout her childhood and on into her adult years.

DADDY'S HOME

More than likely, in most families, the father isn't going to be extremely important during the first year or two of life—not in the same way a mother is. But by the time the child becomes a toddler, Daddy's presence (or that of a father-substitute) is absolutely essential to smooth, continued development.

Carol, the daughter of my friend Lynn, has just turned three. "I go into her bedroom to kiss her goodnight, and she turns her face to the wall," Lynn tells me. " 'I don't want you to kiss me,' " she says. 'I want Daddy.' If Phil's working late, or out at a meeting, Carol doesn't want to go to bed."

Lynn and Phil have a warm, loving marriage. They love their daughter and marvel over her progress. Lynn doesn't feel threatened when her daughter turns away from her. She knows it's a necessary step in growing up, in learning how to separate. But even here, in this family that is in many ways ideal, we can see the problems that can arise if Daddy isn't home—tension, feelings of rejection. Stop to think what it would be like if there were no Daddy in the picture at all.

Like all children, Carol has gone through stages during which she was at risk of being deeply hurt by her mother. First, during birth, she was separated from the fusion with her mother's body. Then she found herself waking up hungry but her mother didn't appear to feed her. Now Carol sees Mommy going off and leaving her in the care of strangers. In observing this bright and personable young girl, I can see that Carol is able to remember the positive aspects of her mother and use those memories to mollify her feelings of hurt and anger. Nonetheless, Carol will still get frustrated occasionally, especially when she's overtired.

Like most other children, at these times Carol turns to her father for comfort. Her father's presence helps divert attention from her mother, and it helps her to retain a more realistic image of her mother. As we saw before, this internal mother image in turn influences how the child perceives other objects in the outside world, and finally how she sees herself. The two parents together provide an extremely important balance.

There's a fable I made up several years ago which illustrates just why that balance is so important.

THE PARABLE OF THE PRISONER

It's the Middle Ages, and I'm a prisoner in a dungeon, a small round room with straw on the floor. Around my leg is a short, thick chain. The door is barred. There's a tiny window high up in the wall, but that's also barred. As far as I know, I'm going to be in this dungeon forever.

I have only one guard. He brings me my food and water. He shovels away the dirty straw and puts down clean straw. This guard controls my life. It's only natural that I hate him.

But I'm also totally dependent on him, so I cannot let him see my hatred. If he knows how much I hate him, he might not come back. He might leave me here alone, and I would die.

As time progresses, I begin to hate myself. Why? Here I am, chained up like a dog and treated like dirt. The only freedom I have is the freedom to *feel*—and the only thing I feel is pure, unalloyed hatred. Yet my very survival depends on my ability to deny that feeling, to chain that monster to my own inner brick walls. Thus I am doubly enchained—once by my captors, and once in a prison of my own devising.

As I said, I am totally dependent on this one person for all my needs. But as I drift off to sleep, I often find myself wishing I had *three* guards. Having three wouldn't make the dungeon any more pleasant. But I could divide up my feelings among these three: I could have one I hate, one that I like, and one whose favor I would curry to help me get out of this prison. With three, the possibility of escape grows. I devise all sorts of plans: I could try to pit the guards against each other. Or perhaps I could whisper malicious gossip to one and provoke him into killing the others. At such moments I feel good about myself—I think I am clever, brave, and vastly superior to these jackals.

Then reality returns. I turn in my sleep, and my clanking chain awakens me. I realize I have just the one guard, and there's nothing I can do except deny my hate, acknowledge my need for him, and pray this despised creature, loathsome as he is, doesn't desert me.

After all, I am wholly dependent on him for my very survival.

The infant, totally dependent on one mother, is like that prisoner with only one guard. She can't afford to get angry at Mother because Mother might leave her, and then what would she do? So she clings. She tries to pretend the "bad" mother doesn't exist, so that she won't get angry. She finds herself in a love/hate relationship with her mother that only grows more frustrating as time goes on. She may even idealize the mother in her effort to deny her frustration.

The father's presence assists the child in breaking away from the mother. He's another person she can direct her love toward, and he's there to absorb some of her anger. When he tends to the child's needs, it helps her realize that Mommy's not the only person who can nurture her. He's there to intercede, to offer another opinion, to balance.

Mother's function is first of all to provide nurturance. The young child is *expected* to be dependent on her. Carol, for example, might insist she wants Daddy to kiss her goodnight, but when she wakes up frightened by spooks in the middle of the night, who's she gonna call? The original Ghostbuster—Mommy, that's who.

The father, on the other hand, provides what's often referred to as "the reality principle." The father, or whoever assumes the father's role, often teaches the child how to fend for herself out there in the world. When the child is seven years old, Daddy is probably the one who'll take the training wheels off the bicycle and run around the block teaching her how to ride. It's the father's role (or, again, whoever assumes the father's role) to introduce you to the world outside the home, to point out its dangers and assist you in overcoming them.

One of the things we've learned about the codependent people we've treated in our program over the past two years—people whose poorly developed sense of themselves has led to failure in forming healthy lasting relationships—is that they all had extremely weak or unavailable fathers. In contrast, our patients usually perceived their mothers as powerful but often overly possessive, or they were hostile to the child, or they were working and were often not available. Early on, the child learned to fear her power. And when the child's relationship with her mother becomes frightening to the child (even if such fears are unfounded), the father's presence is all the more important.

The people who come to us for help are the ones who saw their fathers running away, collapsing under pressure, or cajoling the wife instead of standing up to her, or unavailable because of hostility, sexual promiscuity, or intoxication. As children they realize their fathers couldn't withstand their aggression, that Daddy wouldn't support them against the dangers of the real world. There might have been two parents present, but the child sensed herself totally dependent upon "one guard," and was therefore afraid to get angry or assert herself.

GAIL'S STORY

Gail, a woman I treated at Johns Hopkins, in Baltimore, was someone most people thought of as extremely self-confident. She took a job teaching English in an inner-city school ten or twelve years ago. Walking from the bus stop to the school, she'd notice yet another building that had been boarded up, people selling drugs on the corners, discarded needles in the stairwells of the school, and cars with their windows smashed and wires from their radios hanging loose from the dashboard. But Gail had a mission to teach her third- and fourth-graders, and wasn't about to let herself be frightened. Even when she heard other teachers talking fearfully about finding themselves in the building after five o'clock, she could barely hide her contempt for their fear.

One Thursday she went to a teachers' meeting that ran late, then went back to her classroom to finish the next day's lesson plan. In her rush to get home, she tugged her coat off its hanger and popped the top button. It was almost six-thirty when she headed for the bus stop.

The next thing she knew she was lying on the ground. Her pocketbook was gone, her coat was half off, and she had an unbearable pain in her right side. She ended up in the hospital with two cracked ribs.

One important thing about Gail: She was raised by a single mother and never knew who her father was. Whereas children who grow up with weak fathers often attempt to repress their aggression, those who grow up with a father or strong male figure missing from the picture altogether are frequently unable to recognize aggression—or danger. In order not to offend Mother, their only caretaker, they have to deny any aggression in or toward the mother. In their fantasies, they'll see only the idealized "good" mother, and can only see the idealized "goodness" in the rest of the environment as well. Reality becomes distorted. The child never learns how to test the waters for danger. She might develop a good self-esteem, but her sense of discrimination is sorely lacking. Gail is such a person.

IN RETROSPECT

Obviously, the father's weakness or absence is only part of the picture of codependency. If we look at the number of patients who have sought psychological help, we will certainly find a far greater number raised without strong fathers than we would find in the general population. That doesn't mean that every child raised in a single-parent home will end up suffering from overwhelming emotional problems. There are many other factors, both inside and outside the home, that contribute to the young child's personality development. Most important, perhaps, is the way in which the mother herself handles the delicate life at home.

The love and nurture received first from the mother, then the father, then others in the environment, are crucial. While such love is not enough in itself to assure that the child will grow up able to care for others and able to accept their care in turn, it is the most stable foundation that can be built. There are some children born with so much genetic strength that nothing the parents do will prevent them from asserting themselves and achieving true individuality. Other children, reared in the most stable and nurturing homes, still find themselves unable to break free. As we will see, the majority of people who end up as codependents, unable to form or sustain healthy and satisfying relationships, fall somewhere between these two extremes.

3

The Self Starts

Who are you? What makes you an individual? More precisely, what do you mean when you talk about your *self*?

On one level, the "self" is simply the sum of our parts—the body and the mind. But as you probably suspect, the true definition of self is much more complicated, and our understanding of what constitutes one's self is tangled indeed.

Try to remember what it was like learning to ride a bicycle. As long as the training wheels were attached—no problem. Once those extra wheels were removed, though, you suddenly found yourself struggling to stay upright. You frantically jerked the handlebars, trying—through a combination of instinct, guesswork, and a little bit of panic—to keep the bike under control.

In a sense, our personalities develop the same way. At first our parents serve as "training wheels," holding us up, giving us a sense of freedom, but always there to prevent a disaster. Eventually, though, those "wheels" have to let go. From that moment on the slightest bump in the road through life, or the briefest of momentary lapses in concentration, and we wind up in a heap nursing a skinned knee—or a bruised ego. Some people learn to roll through life with certainty and confidence, and these may be the ones who fly down the street shouting, "Look, Ma, no hands!" Others clutch the handlebars until their knuckles turn white, never able to relax their grip or enjoy the ride.

Our sense of self begins to develop when we first separate

from our parents, specifically our mothers. From that moment on, everything that happens to us—the good, the bad, the somewhere-in-between—contributes something to our personalities. Everything plays a part in determining who we become and how we respond to the world around us: our relationships with our parents and other relatives, our friendships, our activities, our loves and our hates.

The self, then, takes root in infancy, grows throughout childhood and adolescence, and emerges in adulthood armed with certain strengths and limited by certain weaknesses. The exact mix of positive and negative forces is different for each person. And in a way, our personalities are never really fully formed. Throughout our lives, the self is open to subtle and not-so-subtle changes. Aspects of the self may lie hidden for years, then surface later in life in surprising ways.

One more point: When I refer to "selfhood" I am speaking about both the real and the fantasized selves. How we appear to ourselves and how we are perceived by others can be two entirely different things. For example, a person with anorexia may actually weigh only 85 pounds but may perceive herself as grotesquely obese. The picture of her body she has formed in her mind—what we call her internalized body image—is at odds with the facts. Sometimes these two "selves," real and fantasized, can be very different; the wider the chasm between reality and fantasy, the more a person will suffer from a kind of stunted psychological growth, and the shakier the self will be.

Remember Amy, the toddler we met in the last chapter? How she watched other children play? Of course Amy has desires of her own. Because of her mother's holding on and failure to allow Amy to separate, the child thinks she has to suppress those desires so she'll fit her mother's expectations and thus earn her mother's love. The "self" that Amy is developing is a conflicted one; a few years from now, she probably won't be able to tell the difference between what *Amy* wants and what *Mother* wants. She may never be able to stand on her own—or to ride her own psychological two-wheeler. Her concept of self is based upon fantasy and self-deception; she wears more of a "mask" than a "personality."

As the noted psychiatrist Dr. Otto F. Kernberg has stated, to be aware of oneself, by definition, means to be *separate*. Before our distinct self can emerge, we've got to accept our separation from Mother and work to reinforce that separateness.

People who are codependent, however, never really achieved that healthy separation.

THE STAGES OF SEPARATION: A BRIEF OVERVIEW

At the age of five or six months, children make their first incomplete attempts to differentiate themselves from their mother. One year later, as toddlers, the opportunities for greater separation increase. They explore the world around them, assert themselves, say no to Mother, become more interested in Father. The next stage in the process of separation occurs during the Oedipal phase of development, which I'll describe in greater detail in a moment. Later, at nine or ten years of age, children begin forming close friendships outside the home. The last phase of the struggle to break away occurs during adolescence, when children form alliances with their peer group, accepting fads and fashions as alternatives to parental values. Adolescent rebellion is an attempt by teenagers to do anything possible to prove they can function on their own, without parental guidance. Boyfriends and girlfriends, possibly one special boy or girl, will replace the affection that, until now, only the parents could offer.

PUSH, PULL

The healthiest people are those who are best able to manage two conflicting forces in their lives: *dependency* and *aggression*. Dependency is our need for other people, physically and emotionally. This need begins in infancy; in adulthood it takes the form of love, friendship, and sharing.

Aggression balances the scales, making sure we don't become overly dependent and permitting us to develop our strengths as individuals. Without aggressive impulses, without the ability to vent rage on the world around them, children might never be forced to differentiate between themselves and others. But reconciling aggression and dependency can be a struggle, one that will be replayed many times throughout their lives.

One thing we know for certain: We need aggression. Without it there can be no motivation; without motivation, there is no maturity; and without maturity, there can be no healthy sense of self. The need to break away, to assert ourselves, is just as natural to humans as dependency.

THE OEDIPAL PHASE

As we saw in Chapter Two, children become enormously frustrated when they are weaned from the mother's breast and later when they experience separation from Mother. At about the same time this important transition of separation occurs, parents begin to teach children about the importance of cleanliness, particularly the need to use the toilet. In one moment a mother may leave the child with a sitter or a stranger at a day-care center, and in the next breath she may say, "You don't need a diaper—big girls use the potty." The threat of losing Mother is very much on the child's mind and, simultaneously, is what either inspires or intimidates the child's desire to control bowel and bladder.

Thus two major events in a child's life, separation and toilet training, with all their accompanying frustrations and fears, occur at roughly the same period of time. This can be as hard emotionally and physically for a child as it would be for an adult to go through a divorce while moving to a new city and taking on a completely new career. Commonly, children release their frustrations through possessiveness and jealousy. These emotions often signal the onset of the Oedipal phase.

As you probably know, Oedipus was the Greek king who, unaware of his origins, wound up murdering his father and marrying his mother. Infants see Father as little more than an extension of Mother. But during the Oedipal phase of development, sometime between the ages of three and five, little boys begin to see Father in a new light: he becomes their chief rival. Boys feel extremely jealous of the special place Father holds in Mother's heart. At least once in this phase the boy will usually proclaim his intention of marrying his mother. (The flip side, less often articulated, is that the father has to be removed— "killed"—for that union to take place.) While most of us don't take such proclamations very seriously, they nonetheless play an important role in the child's future development. This is, after all, the child's first experience with conscious love for a person of the opposite sex—an experience that will become the model for all future relationships.

All of a sudden, the little boy who used to be so quiet and

good-natured throws a tantrum if Mommy dares to go into the bathroom and close the door. By definition, toilet teaching focuses attention on the child's genitals; the boy learns that his body is different from his mother's, but he's not sure exactly what the difference is. This sense of not knowing can make him feel helpless. He also feels guilty. He recalls his earlier fantasies of attacking his mother's breast; now, however, he's vaguely beginning to experience those same breasts, not as a source of food, but as something strangely new—as sexual objects.

Some therapists and psychiatrists believe that the Oedipal impulses lead to an enormous sense of guilt within an individual. Others, myself included, see guilt as the *cause* of the impulse, not the result of it. Many parents see guilt as a bad thing, something they must help their child avoid at all costs. But guilt has a specific and valuable role in our development as people, in the emergence of the self: It represents the first pangs of *conscience*.

Let me explain. Children sometimes respond to frustration by acting in ways that make them feel guilty. They may bite or scratch; they may break a favorite toy. Immediately afterward, something inside tells them they did something wrong. In turn, these feelings of guilt (fear of losing the important object) motivating them to try and repair the damage and restore the balance in their relationships with the important people and things in their lives. Their early experiences in recognizing—and expressing—such feelings as remorse becomes their model for coping with similar events later in life. The more capably children identify and work through these feelings, the more successful these children will be as adults in their relationships.

ANGELA AND THE BABY

Angela, four years old, lives across the street from me. Almost as soon as she could talk, Angela said she wanted to have a baby sister. Then last summer, as my wife and I sat on the porch, Angela ran over and proudly announced that her mommy was going to have a baby. Bubbling over with joy, she had already decided she would call the baby Jessica. For the next several months, Angela could talk of nothing but Jessica and how they would play together and share Angela's favorite dolls.

But the child was a Jason, not a Jessica. For months after

her brother was born, Angela was sad. She had almost no interest in holding Jason or playing with him. She even had trouble sleeping at night and occasionally experienced bedwetting.

At first her mother dismissed Angela's behavior as disappointment that she didn't get a sister. I told her that while the baby's sex did have something to do with Angela's reaction, there was also a more fundamental problem. Typically, a little boy will experience his growing sexuality as an urge to "replace" his father in his mother's eyes. For a little girl like Angela, however, sexuality may take the form of wanting to have a baby herself—to "replace" the mother or, more specifically, to give birth to her father's child. For a while Angela found her mother's pregnancy to be a source of pleasant fantasy. Once the baby actually appeared on the scene, though, Angela had to deal with the fact that the baby was not really her own. She expressed her disappointment by withdrawing from the baby, by showing no interest in him. If Angela had been a little older, she might have realized earlier in her mother's pregnancy that the expected child would not be hers. She might then have reacted with anger, and might even have fantasized attacking the baby within the mother's womb. As I have indicated, such intense jealousy has a positive side in the growth of the self; it is a powerful source of the competitive spirit that will be beneficial in social encounters later in life. So brother Jason provided our excited Angela with three unexpected blows: the loss of her fantasy to have Daddy's baby; a competition for Mother's attention; and a possible confrontation with knowing the anatomical differences between the sexes.

DADDY'S GIRL

Obviously, little girls like Angela, who fantasize about having babies, will be frustrated in their desires. How a girl deals with this frustration will reflect the way she coped with her earlier frustration, the denial of the mother's breast and later the process of separation.

For example, if the mother and her daughter were able to work through this problem—that is, if the image of the evil woman who refuses to nurse her is reconciled with the image of the loving mother who cares deeply about her child—then the girl will be better able to cope with similar frustrations later in life. If not, there is a risk that the girl will feel impulses, tinged with negativity, that drive her to attach to Mother with hostile ambivalence and be unable to turn to Father for support. Similarly, the father must respect the natural boundaries between himself and his daughter—that is, he must maintain his role as parent and not, of course, as lover. A girl who is unprepared to deal with this natural boundary will perceive that her father is "rejecting" her. (In reality, of course, he is demonstrating his love by maintaining the proper relationship.) In all likelihood, her sense of rejection will affect—and interfere with—her love relationships later in life.

Ideally, the girl emerges from the Oedipal period with her admiration for her father somewhat shaken by the frustrations she's encountered, but she will be emotionally reconciled to the need to wait until she's older before experiencing a healthy love for a man. In later relationships, she can merge the admiration she felt for her father with the excitement and gratitude she experiences at having finally found a legitimate love-object all her own. With her "first love" especially, she desires only to surrender herself, to experience total fusion—which explains why the first love affair is in many ways the deepest and most painful of all. There are a variety of paths and outcomes for all of us as we traverse the Oedipal phase. They demand our attention and clarification, as they provide our original internal representations of our first desires toward someone of the opposite sex.

THE BUDDY SYSTEM

By the time they have passed through the Oedipal stage, most children's personalities are fairly well formed. They realize that they still get much attention from both parents, but they are reconciled to the fact that they are not the "primary love." The parent of the same sex becomes a model; stereotypically, the mother and daughter go shopping together, while the father takes his son to the ball game or coaches his Little League team.

At this age it's a little easier for children to separate their own wants and desires from their parents' expectations. Children form close friendships with their schoolmates, sharing secrets from which the parents are excluded. Girls plead for "sleepovers"; boys love to pass secret messages to each other or make up codes only they can understand. Regardless of the medium of communication, the child's goal is to forge links with peers, and in the process cut the parents "out of the loop."

Separating from parents and striking out on their own is a crucial element of this phase of children's development. As the child psychoanalyst Melanie Klein notes, children who experience a great deal of love in connection with Mother have a lot of love to draw on when forming later attachments. True, the original bond to the parents is diminished somewhat, but no love is really lost; children simply take some of the energy formerly invested in their relationships with their parents and invest it in their new bonds with friends. In doing so they are acting in a healthy manner, following the model given to them by loving parents. However, children from dysfunctional families may never learn how to make or keep friends, since they lack the reservoir of parental love to draw upon. The failure to experience a "buddy" reveals a dysfunctional family and can lead to the future failure of adult codependent relationships.

THE ADOLESCENT

"You're acting like a two-year-old," the mother screams at her teenager. "I've never seen anyone so selfish in my life. You think the whole world revolves around you."

Years of psychological investigation have proved young adolescents go through the same type of emotional turmoil they felt as toddlers. They feel an inflated sense of self-worth and entitlement, viewing their parents and perhaps other people as objects put there merely to gratify their needs.

At this stage, teenagers realize they can't remain attached to their parents forever, but they haven't yet discovered a suitable replacement. So the only option they have is to direct that love toward *themselves*. Because they feel self-conscious about loving their parents, they maintain their distance. They close the door to the bedroom and blast the stereo. They barely say two words during dinner and despise going on family outings. The longer they stay at this point, trying to deny their old attachments to their parents but not ready to set out and find new ones, the more self-centered they will become.

Adolescents at this stage constantly fight the temptation to give up, regress, go back to the point where all they want is their parents' love. Some teenagers, especially boys, protect themselves against regression by continued withdrawal, rejecting anything the parents have to offer—even if it happens to be the thing they want most. A girl is more likely to protect herself by developing an exaggerated crush on a singer, movie star, or teacher. She and her girlfriends *ooh* and *ahh* about this shared idol in the same manner they *ooh* and *ahh* over boys they're attracted to.

"Boys have it so much easier," the teenage girl might complain. "It isn't fair." To an extent, such a lament is a variation of the resentment that many girls feel when they first become aware of anatomical differences. But it also shows that the girl is struggling to deal with the loss of her mother as a love-object and is preparing herself to "compete" with her mother in the sexual arena. In a sense, yes, boys do have it easier: their first feelings of love, from infancy onward, are for a member of the opposite sex, whereas the first person a girl loves is her mother—another woman. Thus a girl must learn not only to separate from her mother but to transform her feelings into love for the opposite sex, an action in which boys have a head start.

At last, though, Johnny gets a steady girlfriend, and Sally has her first serious boyfriend. Their parents sigh with relief that the narcissistic period has finally passed. The kids do their homework together every day after school, go to the movies every weekend. Then all of the sudden, *bam*—the romance is over. Sally comes home sulking and refuses to do anything around the house. Johnny storms into his room and blasts the stereo again. Just when their parents are about to tear their hair out, the kids find romance again. Looking back, we might laugh at the transitory and casual nature of these first romantic attachments; but we are also reminded of the very real and very deep pain we felt when we suffered through similar catastrophes.

Though they seem to have broken the ties to their parents, these teenagers are actually just loosening a few strings; the rope itself remains fastened. In many cases, adolescents don't value their boyfriends or girlfriends for their worth as "people." In a sense, they may be nothing more than objects—or status symbols—someone to idealize and later devalue, or substitutes for the Oedipal love that has been repressed all this time. The typical pattern is: intense, all-or-nothing love; then the anxiety of separation; and finally depression and loneliness. Each time teenagers repeat this cycle, they are subconsciously reenacting the process of giving up the parent. Fortunately, because the pattern gets a little easier with each repetition, most people can usually maintain their new attachments longer.

Not everyone, though. Not people who are unable to reconcile themselves to the loss of their original Oedipal love object, or who are unable to meet the one special person, or who go through one failed relationship after another—in short, not those people who have failed to resolve their dependency/developmental issues. This inability is sometimes, though not always, due to the early influence of a clinging parent.

MY ONE AND ONLY LOVE

Obviously, each child has only one mother. Is it any wonder, then, that children view their mothers as irreplaceable and omnipotent, and that children see themselves as singularly possessing her. Similarly, parents see their children as irreplaceable. But as children grow, they become attracted by events and objects in the world around them. Eventually they surrender their illusion that they alone possess their parents. In contrast, however, many parents do not give up their children so easily.

Let me illustrate by telling you about a young mother named Julie. One day Julie sits on the park bench and watches her four-year-old son, Amos, steal candy from a younger child. She knows what he's doing is wrong, but what is she supposed to do? She doesn't want to embarrass him in front of his friends. Julie has memories of her own mother yelling at her from the window to "straighten up and play nice." She recalls how after that she didn't want to play with the other children for fear they would tease her about being a "Momma's girl." So Julie calls Amos over and suggests they go for ice cream. With his attention diverted, Julie takes the candy out of the boy's pocket and hands it back to the other boy's mother.

I ask Julie why she acted this way. She replied, "I didn't want to criticize Amos. I want him to know I'll love him no matter what he does."

In our conversation we explored this issue further. What advantage is there in valuing a child regardless of his actions? Amos will realize that mother will love him equally under any circumstances. He can clean up his room and help clear the table, or he can steal from a friend and sock a little girl in the nose. It won't matter. This is what we mean by unconditional love, and to a degree, that's a good thing.

But there's a downside. Amos may come to believe that his mother doesn't value him for who he is. Instead, she loves some abstract image—her Son with a capital S. This "Son" might be someone named Johnny or Jamie. It wouldn't matter. By loving him in the abstract, as it were, Julie refuses to acknowledge Amos's separate existence, his unique personality traits, his accomplishments, failures, and frustrations. Amos might come to think, If Mommy loves me whether I'm good or bad, why not go ahead and be bad?

In this case, Amos needs the influence of a strong father to counterbalance the mother; to provide his son with a link to reality and to give him a sense of his obligations to other people and to society. (Keep in mind that in other families the father may be at fault, and the mother may be called on to provide the balance.) Unless there is such an equilibrium, the child's perceptions of what is right and what is wrong are never modified to match the external reality. Protected from the consequences of his actions, he will never manage to internalize the sense of "good" and "bad" that he will need to succeed in life. In other words, he must never wrestle with guilt, and will thus fail to develop a conscience.

We saw before that the link between guilt and conscience is forged before the Oedipal phase. As their children grow, good parents consciously use guilt to help them adjust to social rules. With maturity, conscience takes the place of guilt. Mother doesn't have to make Jimmy feel bad that he hit his sister; he feels bad enough already. Guilt, in this instance, is external; conscience is internal. In the normal progression to adulthood, conscience—our internalized authority figure—makes us stop and think before we act. Relationship destruction in adult life due to *adultery* is one example of poorly internalized parenting.

CELEBRATING OURSELVES

I celebrate myself
And what I assume you shall assume
For every atom belonging to me as good belongs to you.
　　　　　—Walt Whitman, "Song of Myself"

Adolescence is traditionally the time for working through the final conflicts with Oedipal relations, trying out romantic love, and preparing ourselves for mature love. How we feel about ourselves at the end of adolescence will in turn influence what we can bring to another person in a loving relationship, as well as what we expect from them. Only when we feel good about who we are—when we can celebrate ourselves—are we able to appreciate the individuality and special traits in others.

Many people, unfortunately, pass through adolescence without developing a mature sense of themselves as individuals. So what do they do now? How can they compensate for their early failures?

As we'll see in the chapters that follow, often these people plunge into unsuitable marriages or move in with the first lover who'll agree to share closet space with them, or with someone who is "good in bed." Subconsciously these people are telling themselves, I'm going to pick somebody that I really don't like, and I'll lie to myself about how wonderful that person is. Then I'll use this person to escape from having to live with my parents, or to escape from my loneliness, or whatever my current situation is. But I'm going to treat this person in the way I never had nerve to treat my parents. When I do that I'll get my revenge. I'll find the sense of separateness that I need so badly, and that my parents never gave me.

You see the problem: All the energy that this person brings to the relationship is focused on being *destructive*. Quite predictably, that person is going to find it pretty difficult to love someone else and have that love endure. This is the person who becomes trapped in a destructive codependent relationship.

4

The Sexual Self

Laura comes into my office on Monday morning. When I ask how her weekend was, she says, "It was fabulous."

"Why do you say that?" I ask.

"Because," she replies with a smile, "I had great sex."

I ask her what she means. Laura explains: "We went to dinner in a candlelit restaurant. Very romantic—and the food was good. Then we went to my place and had a long conversation. We talked about the way the seasons change, and how the way a child looks at Nature is so different from the way an adult does. Then we took turns choosing favorite record albums and telling each other why we thought the music was particularly special. Then we played a game: He pointed to things in the room—a painting or a book or something—and asked me to tell him the story how it happened to be there. Eventually we went to bed, but we still talked for a while and cuddled for a long time before we made love. Then, still holding each other, we fell asleep."

Look carefully at what Laura is saying—or rather, what she is *not* saying. She didn't describe great sex as "endless hours of incredible sexual acrobatics" or "the most mind-boggling multiple orgasms I've ever had." Instead Laura is describing the experience of sharing beautiful things—food, music, thoughts—with a person she cares about.

When people speak of sex, they generally mean the physical relationship between two people. But "sex"—intercourse— is only a small part of sexuality. Sexuality, the magnetism that attracts people to each other so they may form relationships, is made up of a lifetime of experiences, feelings, and thoughts; it involves our responses to the people and events around us. We bring all these experiences with us when we fall in love. In short, sex is physical; sexuality is physical, emotional, even spiritual.

SEXUAL BEGINNINGS

Sexuality isn't something we suddenly switch on when we want to hop into bed with someone and that we switch off when the sex act is done. It's a deeply rooted part of our whole being, a part that grows and matures inside each person in much the same way that the ego or personality develops.

The process of forming a sexual identity begins the moment a mother takes her infant in her arms. The first two sensual pleasures the infant becomes aware of are the warmth of being held and the gratification of being fed. Being fed, however, is connected with sucking the mother's breast, a process with numerous sensual undertones. The warm stream of milk runs down the throat into the stomach, creating another sensual experience.*

The look in the mother's eyes, the quality of her smile, the way in which the mother touches, nurses, caresses, and kisses affects the way the baby responds to bodily contact. As the mother changes the diaper, she naturally must clean her baby's genitals in the process. The way she touches these parts—even the names she gives to them—will subtly reflect how she views both her own and her infant's sexuality. In a sense, her actions silently communicate some aspects of her relationships with the baby's father. Then, when the father holds the infant in his arms, the impressions the baby gets confirm or deny the signals from the mother. Thus, from earliest infancy, the child of either sex is experiencing sensual ties to *both* parents.

Through all these ministrations, parents may promote the child's acceptance of his or her own body, or they may

---

*The breast symbolizes the infant's sensual experience of gratification, accompanied by being held, along with the warmth, security, and love that occurs with breast or bottle feeding.

inadvertently transmit a body image that is fragile and devoid of sensuality. Memory of the tender touching of the erogenous zones that the infant experienced in his or her mother's arms will play a role throughout life. The "loved enough" grown person will seek partners who can provide the same stimulation and satisfaction. Others seek one who can provide only what was primarily lacking; for example, the need to be held and touched is sought while intercourse is tolerated only as a means of being held and touched. Or, more extreme, there are the adults who, due to the frustrations experienced in their mother's arms, cannot stand being touched, avoid eye contact, and resist taking pleasure in touching their own genitals.

As we saw in Chapter Two, when the mother is not physically present, the infant will seek objects that offer similar gratification. Research has shown that, when the mother-child relationship is at its best, children usually begin to play with their genitals before the age of one. Where the relationship is problematic, other objects, separate from the body, draw the infant's attention. This genital play during the first two years of life is *not* masturbation or an attempt to achieve erotic stimulation. Instead it simply represents the child's simple effort to recreate the mother's pleasurable attentions.

"LITTLE BOY" AND "LITTLE GIRL"

New mothers often dress the baby girl in pink, the boy in blue; if they didn't, strangers probably wouldn't know the difference. Neither, for that matter, does the infant. During the baby's first two years of life, sexual distinctions are more important to other people than they are to the baby. Boys and girls alike identify with the mother and want to become like the mother, an urge that often includes the desire to have a baby. Because the infant depends on the mother (and particularly the mother's breast), she appears omnipotent. If children are ever going to move away from this frightening image of the mother, they must find an alternative source of comfort. Usually, this means turning to the father.

Between 12 and 18 months, most toddlers become aware that Father's body is different from Mother's. They perceive the father's penis as an "object" in much the same way that the mother's breast is an "object"—something separate from the "whole" body. As we discussed in Chapter Two, most children at this age are weaned and attention begins to focus on toilet training. Children perceive this event as a shift in attention from Mommy's breast to their own genitals. Remember that at this stage the little boy continues in his love for his mother. Later he will want to marry her and want her to have his child, but he will realize he has a powerful rival: his father. The little girl will begin directing her love to the father, and later will want to give birth to the father's baby.

What both the boy and the girl are actually experiencing at this stage is a profound desire to return to the mother's womb (a oneness with the one who loves them.) The innate memory of life in the womb—a time of total fusion, safety, and absence of frustrations—offers a tempting fantasy, one that contrasts sharply with the natural, and unpreventable, next step of separating from Mother. The intense desire for reunion triggers an early stage of the separation struggle. For a brief time, the child perceives anything that stands in the way of returning to the womb as representing the "bad" father.

Again, during this time, we often observe children fondling their genitals. The difference is that now they are consciously trying to stimulate themselves. This ability to give oneself pleasure eases the trauma of setting forth on one's own, and signals the child's beginning to take possession of his own body. Studies indicate that when children are overly anxious about Mother's whereabouts, they show less interest in genital play.

LIKE MOTHER, LIKE DAUGHTER

By definition, a girl going through the Oedipal period is jealous of her mother. But, as we saw in Chapter Three, when the parents' relationship is good, a girl who turns to her father is rewarded with kisses and hugs—her first experience of caresses from a person of the opposite sex. Once again, how the mother views her own sexuality is of primary importance. Under the best conditions, the girl turns to her father not so much because the mother has disappointed her, but because she wants to be like her mother. If the mother has not resolved her own conflicts about the usefulness of the female genitals, or if she attempts to avoid touching the little girl, the girl will not develop a positive sense of herself with which to appeal for her father's love. As we said earlier, she remains excessively attached to the mother, experiencing a hostile ambivalence about her dependency.

Unconsciously, the "Breast-Mother" in this excessive attachment situation will always be *responsible for all* of the baby's pleasure and *all* of its pain. As babies, children fantasize attacking the mother's absent breast and devouring the depriving mother (reflecting the child's innate aggression). Later, as a girl enters the Oedipal stage, she might fantasize about destroying a baby in her mother's womb so that she can create the baby herself. As the Oedipal stage progresses, the girl closely identifies her own body with that of her mother; her sense of guilt may be greater than a boy experiences. She becomes anxious that mother will retaliate and rob her of all the "good" things inside her.

If you feel that the level of aggression that I describe is excessive, well, I can both understand your reaction and also assure you that infant observational research has repeatedly confirmed this childhood aggression. Indeed, aggression in response to anxiety is central to human life and relationships.

Such anxiety in children, if extreme and if not balanced by a strong image of the "good" mother, will often prompt a little girl to be overly concerned with her appearance. She seems to think that by having unusually long hair or putting on certain clothes she can somehow repair the fantasized "damage" she has done to her mother's body and to her own. Unconsciously, this concern with physical appearances follows many women well into adulthood. In other cases, a child's anxiety about harming the mother's body and her fear of retaliation may cause her to become a "tomboy"; often, such children grow up feeling hatred or revulsion for their capacity to become mothers—the very capacity that, as toddlers, they valued so highly.

GIVING MOMMY CHILDREN

Before too long, the little boy begins to urinate standing up. From this point on, his genitals will become associated with excitement and aggression. At around two and a half to three years, the boy begins to identify his own genitals with his father's. "Look at this, look what I have. I can marry Mommy and give her a baby, just like Daddy did." But a boy could express such thoughts in many different tones of voice: joy,

STUMBLING BLOCKS

Trouble arises if the mother is overly possessive in caring for her son or if she secretly desires him as a kind of replacement for his father. Such mothers will subconsciously convey the message that the boy's infantile sexuality is enough to satisfy her.

The danger is that a boy in these circumstances will sense he doesn't need to turn to the father, and won't have to learn from him or admire him. In most cases this means the boy will grow up overvaluing his own worth and embracing a distorted concept of sexuality (perversions). He may ignore the necessary boundaries between the generations and may possibly ignore the differences between men and women as well. He is likely never to feel envy for anyone else and will never feel the need to seek a love relationship that allows him to unite with the femininity he gave up when he separated from his mother's body. Femininity, which involves the whole woman, is neither desired nor appreciated. Sexually, he seeks parts of a woman, her "great tits" or "great ass," her long blond hair, etc. Emotionally, he seeks the weak or vulnerable woman—one he can *control*.

delight, superiority, or anger. The inflection he chooses depends upon three things: the father's relationship with the mother (as the little boy perceives it); the boy's ability to retain the image of the "good breast" (even though the breast is now denied him); and his ability to merge that image with the image of the "good penis" (to identify with the loving father.) When the good images predominate, the boy can see his bodily parts, like those of his father, as gifts that can give the mother pleasure. When the "bad breast" and the "bad penis" remain uppermost in his mind, he perceives the father as penetrating and harming his mother; such thoughts remind the boy of his original desire to harm the depriving or absent breast. He becomes anxious that father will retaliate. This anxiety leads to what psychoanalysts call the "castration complex." The boy might become so anxious about castration that his loses his ability to derive pleasure from genital self-stimulation and turns to alternative

The healthy feminine woman will be experienced as too aggressive. He's rarely going to experience guilt or develop the sense that he must repair any damage he causes. Yet anxiety, guilt, and sadness normally motivate a person to try and repair the damage, and are thus essential to the emotional life of any child—not just for sexual development but to create healthy relationships with the world around them. Emotional and sexual development thus go hand in hand.

The little girl who is loved too dearly by her father, who appears to be taking the place of the mother in the parents' relationship, is also likely to have problems later in life. Her first love was for her mother, someone of her own sex, a love that ultimately proved frustrating. On top of that, she can never be sure she'll be enough to satisfy Daddy—after all, Mother wasn't enough; that's why Daddy turned to the little girl. A little boy who is overly prized by his mother since birth becomes grandiose, narcissistic, and reverted; in contrast, a little girl who is excessively prized by her father can't be sure about anything and continually doubts herself, as she participates in confusing adult love/hate relationship failures.

behaviors—biting fingernails, playing with his nose or ears, twirling hair, or developing uncontrollable tics.

In every little boy, the understanding of the good penis and its ability to give pleasure develops side by side with castration fears. Under the best circumstances, his relationship with the good father will allay his fears and allow his sexual development to proceed normally. The good image he retains of his body translates into good impressions of the world around him. He comes to trust his ability to repair the damage he may have done, or to assuage fear, so he needs no longer fear either his desires or his potency.

SOCIAL NORMS

To illustrate how sexuality develops and how social standards affect that development, let me trace the changes as they occur in two hypothetical, but nonetheless representative, children.

Janet is three years old; her brother Vic has just turned five. Janet watches as Vic and the boys he plays with run into the bathroom, competing to see who can send the best jetstream into the toilet. Janet feels bad that she can't join them.

One night, as Vic gets undressed for bed, Mommy comes in and catches him playing with himself. "You're really growing up, aren't you," Mommy said, kissing him and tucking him into bed.

Now Janet's really confused. She remembers a few weeks ago Mommy caught her fondling her genitals and gave her a big lecture: "You nasty girl! That's a filthy thing to do! You should never touch yourself there!"

If you were Janet, you'd probably be confused, too. Yet Janet's mother acted precisely as our society dictates. Some physicians and educators warn parents that they shouldn't interfere with masturbation in boys, but they should discourage it in girls at all costs. Our society's double standards in dealing with sexual stereotypes is apparent, even in children as young as Vic and Janet.

One way this difference manifests itself is in a child's dreams. Often Vic will have dreams about replacing Daddy or being just like Daddy. He seems to be aware in a vague way that his genitals are involved in these desires.

Janet's dreams are more "creative" than her brother—at least in her parents' view. She often wakes and tells Mommy that during the night she imagines herself floating or flying. In classic dream analysis, such dreams, in which the person's body appears to lose all its weight, are considered extremely feminine. Sometimes, in other dreams, Janet is alone; sometimes she's dancing with her parents and all their friends are admiring her. The little girl who is still going through a difficult Oedipal crisis might have fears about being kidnapped or "robbed." Like other brothers and sisters their age, Janet and Vic sometimes explore each other's bodies. Usually this activity is limited to looking and touching, but some children go so far as to attempt a kind of intercourse. Vic sees his sister as a stand-in for Mommy, and Janet sees her brother as Daddy's substitute; since their parents have physically denied them, this is the best they can do. Few children pass through the Oedipal stage without "playing doctor" once in a while; for some children, however, the experience produces severe feelings of guilt. Such children feel they deserve to be punished for attempting to replace their parents, the real object of their curiosity, and if they don't get help overcoming this guilt, they could remain stagnated at this phase of development. At its worst, a crisis of this sort may cause a child to become involved in a repeating cycle of dangerous sexual situations.

OTHER INTERESTS

Janet, now five years old, is starting to explore her world more vigorously. "Don't ride your brother's bike," Janet's mother tells her. "You'll hurt yourself." Janet's mother never says exactly how she might get hurt. But Janet knows it has something to do with that bar running from the seat to the handlebars; she also suspects it has something to do with that part of her body she's not supposed to touch or talk about— her "secret place." So Janet contents herself with riding her own bike, sliding down ropes and an occasional banister when she visits her grandparents; she jumps rope steadily and rhythmically.

Many parents like to assume that their children's sexual instincts simply disappear around the time they enter school. At the same time these parents become aware that their children are suddenly unable to sleep through the night, or have developed complex rituals centered around undressing and going to bed. The children seem easily bored, or less spontaneous in play than before. Typically, parents dismiss these personality changes; they'll say, "Oh, it's probably because Johnny has just entered school," or "Sally is developing so many new interests," or "Lucinda is tense about being away from home all day for the first time." Parents usually don't connect these changes with the fact that children in this stage are attempting to suppress the fantasies usually associated with masturbation. For years to come, those fantasies may be suppressed as the children focus on learning, on developing new skills and interests. But their bodily instincts don't simply "disappear." They'll reemerge sometime—and in some way.

BODILY CHANGES

As he approaches puberty, Vic becomes more open about his masturbation. As he gets older he'll compare notes and openly discuss his masturbation fantasies with his friends.

Janet is less likely to engage in mutual sex play with friends (although many girls do), since in her mind her genitals are still connected with mystery and with bodily excretions.

The best she can do is form an idealized image of her smooth, round body, with its growing breasts and excitable nipples. Instead of fantasizing about her physical prowess, she dreams of Prince Charming, love, marriage, and having her own children. Some psychiatrists have suggested that, because her sexual development is more self-contained, it requires more courage. They contend that the loneliness she experiences now increases her later ability for a strong commitment to a relationship.

As we saw in Chapter Three, until puberty a girl will probably be closer to her mother, while a boy will hopefully be pals with his father. One of the tasks of early adolescence is to diminish this bond and learn how to transfer romantic thoughts to a partner of the opposite sex. Exactly how adolescents accomplish this task will depend on their experiences during the Oedipal period, when the children first turned away from the parent of the same sex. As with Janet and Vic, the awareness that the parent is unavailable at this stage often leads to sex play between brothers and sisters, or between playmates. A similar process takes place in adolescence; this time, however, the partner is first fantasized then becomes real. If proper care isn't taken, the "sex play" might be for keeps—complete with unwanted pregnancy and an earlier-than-wanted experience of relationship failure.

LOVE ROMANTICIZED

At the age of twelve, Janet and her girlfriends develop a crush on Michael Jackson, going to all his concerts, swaying in rhythm with his songs. Such bodily movements parallel younger girls jumping rope, providing both stimulation and the discharge of energy. Janet's old enough now to understand the sexual content of her movements. And she'll blatantly admit she's "in love" with Michael Jackson. She is narcissistically staking her claim on him, perhaps imagining him looking out into the audience and selecting her as the object of his attentions. At this point, her concept of "love" is still more tied to affection, or being admired than it is to intercourse.

Janet is experiencing what we call *pregenital* love—abstract love that does not involve shared genital stimulation. At this stage, a girl's every concept of love reflects the experience of fusion with her mother's body or tenderness of the infant held in the mother's arms. Pregenital love will always remain perfect, more sensual than physical, more a product of sexuality than of sex.

At school, Janet is as demonstrative in her gestures toward boys in her sixth-grade class as she is at the Michael Jackson concert. At twelve, most of the boys in her class are still psychologically uneasy in responding to her affections. Having been more open in genital play until this point, boys experience more conflict at breaking from the Oedipal, incestual fantasies of their mother's love. Being on the defensive, Vic is more apt to say that girls—those in his class, but his mother and sister, too—"disgust" him.

Pregenital love is a phase that both boys and girls go through, and which usually passes at some point during early adolescence. If it is not successfully conquered as a teenager, it is bound to interfere with future relationships. Adult love that remains affectionate and sensual but devoid of genital desire results in impotence. Until the adult rediscovers the fusion offered by genital, sexual union, that person remains tied to feelings of narcissistic entitlement that first arose in infancy. In selfish pursuit of orgasm, and unable to communicate physically through intercourse, such a person might just as well masturbate; in fact, excessive masturbation or the need for multiple sex partners with whom the physical relationship is limited to the eroticized sexual play is often a problem for people caught up in the cycle of romanticized, unfulfilled love. As Sigmund Freud said, we can only use the word "love" when a mutual and complementary genital component has come into play in the relationship.

SELF-FULFILLMENT

Earlier we saw how genital stimulation aids toddlers' sense of themselves. Remember, too, that children who feel overly unprepared about setting forth on their own often show no interest in genital play. The same cycle repeats at puberty, when masturbation once again becomes a conscious act. Each child *must,* at this stage, develop a sense of himself or herself as a separate, sexual being. One's body belongs to oneself; manipulating one's own body for self-pleasure is in essence staking a rightful claim. Adolescents who do not masturbate are unwilling or unable to take charge of the physical sensations arising within themselves. For example, take a girl in particular who has developed the habit of repressing masturbation. If as an adolescent she still doesn't want to break away from home—if she still wants to see herself primarily as Mommy's friend or Daddy's darling—she'll probably repress her urges to masturbate at this stage as well. In adult relationships, her pleasure (or misery) will remain the *others'* responsibility.

Masturbation also helps the child make the necessary transition from romantic, pregenital love, to full genital, sexual enjoyment. But when teenagers are still closely and ambivalently attached to their parents and are overly anxious about breaking those ties, masturbation—even as an intermediate step in sexual development—might not provide sufficient proof of their sexual capacity. The risk here is that such children engage in heterosexual activity far too soon. Sex on these terms takes place before the adolescent is prepared to deal with its physical and emotional consequences. Considered in this light, masturbation among teenagers often represents a more mature and desirable choice as a form of sexual self-expression.

FIRST FANTASIES

When adolescents learn to derive stimulation and excitement from their own bodies, the fantasies that accompany this act helps them develop healthy images of themselves. These fantasies take participants to an altered state of consciousness in which the ego relinquishes much of its control. And like dreams, fantasies often reveal more about the *self,* and the relationship between children and their parents, than they do about anything sexual.

Janet recalls a fantasy she had around the time she began to menstruate: "I walk into the bathroom and find my brother's closest friend taking a shower. He steps out of the shower and reaches for a towel, but as he does that he puts his arm around me. He stands there naked, and I begin to explore his body. He reaches under my skirt and fondles my 'secret place' through my panties." Janet says she never realized how good such contact could feel. She adds that, in her fantasy, she knows her brother is waiting outside the door. He's not looking through the keyhole but he knows what's going on. Janet says she knows he's happy for her, too.

Let's explore this fantasy and see what it means. To do so

we must first "desexualize" it. In her fantasy, Janet walks into the bathroom and is surprised—but not frightened. What happens between her and her brother's friend is as innocent as the sex play between two children, but it makes her feel good. When she says she knows her brother is happy for her, too, she's proving that she has a good self-image, that she feels good about herself and trusts her own instincts and happiness. She's also chosen someone in her own age group, someone she could conceivably become healthily involved with.

Let's contrast Janet's situation with Marilyn's. Her first fantasy involved "Uncle Harry," her father's friend from childhood who is a frequent visitor to their house. In her fantasy, Marilyn is swimming with Uncle Harry at the lake by their summer cabin. He takes off his bathing suit and convinces her to do the same. They start touching each other in the water. Then he holds her from behind, as if he's going to teach her how to float on her stomach. He's manipulating her legs and genitals. At first it feels good, but then Marilyn feels frightened, believing that she's going to start having trouble breathing, maybe even drown.

Marilyn's fantasy shows intense fear, an inability to trust herself or to let herself take pleasure in the experience without suffering consequences suggesting that she has not successfully separated from mother. One more note: The fact that Marilyn chooses her father's closest friend as partner can be interpreted as revealing the girl's unresolved Oedipal conflicts with her father. Marilyn does not experience orgasm in her masturbation attempts and may very well end up in adult life picking a cold and crude sexual man whom she can blame for her lack of sexual satisfaction.

HOW THE FANTASIES WORK

In Chapter Three we saw how adolescents often become self-centered when they attempt to break away from the parents yet are still unable to form relationships with their peers. The same is true of the masturbation fantasies accompanying early adolescence. During the Oedipal phase, children's fantasies center on Mommy or Daddy; during early adolescence, fantasies usually center on the self and on the attachments that the younger child felt regarding a parent. But the purpose of puberty is to reveal the usefulness of the genitals in procreation while helping orient the child toward suitable partners of the opposite sex. Through fantasy, through masturbation, young men and women learn to develop a healthy masculine or feminine image of themselves.

At some point during adolescence, young people progress from the infantile experience of *being* loved (being cuddled in Mommy's arms, simply surrendering to the affections of another) to the experience of *giving* love (trusting the love within oneself and feeling both the need and the desire to share it with another person). The masturbation fantasy aids young people in harnessing this self-love and directing it outward. They *fantasize* closeness to another person before they actually *become* close.

MOTHER, SON, AND THE "OTHER" WOMAN

In sixth grade, Vic is afraid to show any interest in women. Remember, girls "disgust" him. Though he won't admit it, he has divided women up into "good" and "bad" (translation: "asexual" and "sexual"). And though he'll cross the street to avoid passing the sexiest girl in the school, she's likely to be the one he fantasizes about while he masturbates. Once he gets over the fantasy, he might fantasize someone a little less sexy, until gradually the girls in his fantasies are closer to reality— that is, the girls he'll stop and talk to. Through repeated fantasies, repeated conversations with girls, and the onset of dating, he gradually relaxes his defenses.

Even when he begins to date one girl steadily, she's probably not going to be the object of his fantasies. Romantic love is highly idealistic; Vic feels he mustn't "degrade" his girlfriend by thinking about her in a sexual way. For him, Mother is still the ideal woman, and his image of the girl he loves must be gently caressed and protected as he would protect his mother. If he happens to find himself alone with his girlfriend in a situation that could become sexual, he becomes distressed and doesn't know what to do. Normally, under these circumstances, the adolescent relives the original separation trauma, and learns to unite good and bad in his images of one person. That's good, because it means tenderness, affection, and pregenital love coexist with genital love in one and the same person. The tender woman and the sexual woman unite. Bingo: Vic develops the capacity to love a girl from his own generation, without feeling as if he is betraying his Oedipal first love.

LOVE CONTINUED

Of course you loved your parents. But before you understood "love" you understood "dependency." You knew that if your mother wasn't there to feed you, you might die of hunger. Let's look again at how the original dependency need was transformed into what you now think of as "love":

After her children are born, Mother has just one goal: to love her babies and to demonstrate her love by holding, feeding, changing them, and keeping them warm. Mother and child share the same goal. Later, though, infants must eventually experience the pain of *not* being loved—not being held at just the right moment, not being fed when hunger pangs strike. Young children turn this pain, this perceived rejection, into a new feeling: aggression or, more specifically, *hate*. But all of a sudden Mother enters the room, lifts the infant from the crib, cuddles, and offers the breast. Suddenly the child feels *grateful*. Now, instead of seeing their mother as an object to absorb hate, children start to appreciate the differences between her body and their own. From this point on, children start wanting to duplicate this event. *They want to love another person actively;* they want to fulfill that person's need in the same way their mother tends to their needs.

We humans are pair-bonded creatures. After all, Noah took two of every creature onto the Ark. Though we spend years trying to separate, to "find ourselves" as self-sustaining individuals, we must not neglect our innate need to share life with another person. In adults lucky enough to have well-structured personalities, their love for their parents does not disappear. Instead it spreads out, strengthening their connections to their partners. Our continuing need to "find ourselves" becomes the couple's search for a shared—and healthy—identity.

Sexual identity adds depth to our mature selves. When we allow genital love to enter a relationship, we finally move from the act of "falling in love" to the state of "being in love." At that point our ability to identify with another person deepens; we transform our idealized visions into a commitment to a living, breathing reality.

But if during the separation and Oedipal phase of our growth, love took on too many of the wrong kinds of sexual overtones; if as we try to learn how to love other people we must deny too many feelings rooted in our past relationships with our parents, then the split between romanticized love and sexual desires may never be healed. As a psychotherapist, I believe that many people—more than we perhaps care to admit—carry damaging remnants of their past with them as they try to forge adult relationships. If this "baggage" isn't jettisoned at the right time, those relationships—those *codependent* relationships—are doomed to fail with considerable pain and destruction.

5

What Makes a Mature Relationship?

Over lunch, my friend Ray is bragging about Evelyn, his latest love.

"Wait till you meet her," he beams. "I've never met anyone so dynamic. She's head of the personnel department over at the bank, works incredibly hard, and yet still really takes care of herself. She combines everything I've ever wanted in a woman—brains, sex, stability. You name it and she's got it. When we're together it's magic, sheer magic!"

"Sounds perfect," I remark.

"Well, I don't want to overstate it. We have our differences. She hates Italian food," Ray said as he wound another mouthful of spaghetti onto his fork. "And she was married once before. That bothers me a little. And I wish she didn't have two children. That's a big stumbling block. But they seem like good kids. With Evelyn for a mother, they'd *have* to be."

Sigmund Freud said that, for a man, "Being in love means greatly exaggerating the difference between one woman and another." In mature coupling, a person selects another who is not only unique, but who returns the love in a unique manner. This is the closest we will ever come to that original fusion I described earlier—that full possession of the mother, which we give up in separating and which we have longed for ever since. Finding that one special person to love above all others is, in effect, paradise regained.

After we pass successfully through the Oedipal phase we have achieved a certain amount of maturity. Before we can select one special partner and set them apart in their uniqueness, we've got to be able to tolerate ambivalence, to realistically balance the person's good and bad qualities.

Until Ray got to the point about Evelyn's children, I worried that he wasn't seeing the whole picture, but his realization that this might be a drawback suggested to me that he might have everything in perspective.

BEING DEPENDENT TOGETHER

Codependency is the study of relationships. Look at the word itself: *co*dependency. We find that same "c-o" combination at the beginning of the word "couple." When you select one person and say, "I want to spend the rest of my life with you," you're going to have to learn to share. Mature coupling involves shared dependency and shared aggression. And let's hope you've successfully integrated sexual passion with the mature desire to love and be loved. Otherwise your relationship is at a very high risk of failing.

Being dependent together can be a very beautiful thing. On the other hand, codependency can be extremely destructive. An adult relationship poses a twofold challenge: to maintain and enhance your own identity while sharing yourself with another person. An author on codependency defined love as "enhancement." I like that word. But holding onto your sense of yourself while you transcend the self in fusion with the person you love is exciting—and painful.

COMMITMENTS

Falling in love is easy—we all know people who do it once a week. *Staying* in love is the hard part.

A mature relationship means being able to appreciate another person's strengths without exaggerating them. Through a process of mutual respect and appreciation, each person also develops a better relationship to his or her own self. Perhaps the most valuable aspect of the mature relationship is that it releases the creative potential within each individual.

The trouble is, we often have trouble establishing and maintaining such relationships. Think about it: How many couples do you know who have a stable relationship based upon mutual respect? Probably pretty few, if any at all. Why should that be the case? That's what the study of codependency is all about.

No species remains dependent on others of its kind longer than humans do. Even as adults with children of our own, we are expected to love, honor, and respect our parents. In a mature relationship, healthy dependency is expressed as *concern,* and concern leads to *commitment.* Commitment means we're willing to let ourselves play an important role in another person's life but that we won't attempt to control that person. Making a commitment does not imply that everything will progress smoothly from this point on. Even in the best relationships, people inadvertently hurt and are hurt. But, as Melanie Klein has observed, the trust in one's ability to *make reparation* for these hurts is a prerequisite to commitment.

REASSURANCES

In her article "Hate, Greed, and Aggression" analyst Joan Riviere explored the motives behind a couple's decision to marry. She found that the need for reassurance about one's personal value often plays a larger role in that decision than feelings of love or even of sexual desire. One of the advantages of healthy codependence, according to Riviere, is "that [one person] is full of a love which can satisfy and fulfill the needs of another...."

This becomes apparent when we trace the sexual personality of the couple back to the individual partners' Oedipal fears and frustrations. For example, recall that a little girl might fantasize attacking her mother's breast, then later worry that the "badness" inside her would damage her beloved father. Her own sexual organs become not just secret, but dangerous. Later, when she becomes genitally involved with her lover, this girl might at first worry for his safety; soon, though, she sees she is able to give him pleasure. In a mature relationship, each person's sense of his or her own "goodness" is continually being questioned and then confirmed—hence the reassurance that typifies a mature relationship. Without this questioning, if the aggressive tendencies inherent in our sexual natures are repressed, so is the love that flows from the reassurance of our "goodness."

A LITTLE SELF-TEST

Read the following list of words:

A. ONENESS
B. SAMENESS
C. LIKENESS
D. CLOSENESS

Think about these words carefully. What does each one mean? They seem very similar, don't they? But as you consider them, you begin to realize the subtle differences among them.

Now for a pop quiz: Which of the words in that list *best describes* what "being dependent together" means to you?

Don't hurry; there's no time limit. In fact, the longer you take to answer, the better your choice will be. Choose your answer before reading further.

Now let's look at what your answer reveals.

A: Oneness People who choose this answer tend to look for relationships that recapture the same feeling of ambivalent attachment they had with their mothers back when they were infants. Sure, there's comfort to be had from such fusion, in surrendering oneself totally to another, but it's a childish kind of comfort; we become unique and powerful. If you crave oneness with another person you have a weak sense of yourself. You are looking for someone to take care of you; may feel deeply anxious unless you know that someone is available to tend to your every need. People who value Oneness in a relationship are guaranteed to become codependent.

B: Sameness People who seek a partner in whom they

COMMUNION

Listen to Lisa, who is getting back on her feet after her divorce: "Well, I'll say this much—I've never been able to concentrate on my work as well as I did during the first few years of my marriage. Just knowing that Geoff and I would be having dinner together, that I wouldn't have to eat alone and see Sameness crave a kind of magical identification with that person. People often use such relationships to confirm that they are worthwhile individuals—"I can't be crazy or stupid; there's another person who sees things the same way I do"—and thus feel better about themselves. The danger in craving Sameness is that you may end up idealizing your partner. You're also likely to deny the differences between yourself and another person, and will blame and criticize them for things that are really wrong with yourself.

C: Likeness   People who choose this are on the right track. They're eager to identify with their mates, but must remember to maintain the differences between them and keep those differences in proper perspective. Of course, it's good if you can form bonds with people who share your likes and dislikes. The downside is that you may start placing so much value on how "alike" you and your partner are that you become unaware of the differences between you. Often, when Likeness is the highest goal in a relationship, people fall apart when the necessary—and inevitable—differences emerge.

D: Closeness   That's the magic word. Closeness means that two people get as near as possible to one another, but still preserve their unique identities. More than likely, an individual who desires to be close to another person, but without being "like" that person or the "same," will be more able to form healthy relationships. They are separate, but not completely alone. If you strive for Closeness, you will achieve a healthy codependent relationship that is personally rewarding and mutually gratifying. The desire for a lasting relationship will be appreciated more than any individual need to feel unique.

wouldn't have to sleep alone, enabled me to devote all my attention to the projects before me."

Here's Gretchen, still radiant after six months of marriage: "Sometimes I think the hardest part about being single and alone was the burden I was placing on my friends, especially the ones who were married. My friends were wonderful, I don't mean to imply anything else, but I felt as if I was clinging desperately to them through every crisis I experienced. And it wasn't fair, because I wasn't reciprocating. I was dependent on them, but if they went through a crisis, they had their wives or their husbands to turn to. Instinctively I knew that I couldn't rely on them forever—not if they were going to remain my friends."

Besides confirming our "goodness," a relationship at its best means that loneliness is banished forever—at least, as long as the relationship lasts. As mature adults in a healthy relationship, we take turns fulfilling each others' needs, and we do so because we are convinced we'll never again have to endure the trauma of separation.

A TALE OF TWO COUPLES

Marc is a stockbroker in a large brokerage house. It's a high-pressure job to begin with, and since the first of the year the market has been slowly declining. Each morning Marc drives to work with his friend Dennis, who also works at the brokerage. This morning their conversation focuses on their belief that something is about to happen to the market. Sure enough, the Dow Jones average is off another ten points at closing; frustrated customers have been calling since one o'clock.

Quitting time comes at last. Marc calls home, as he usually does, to say he's leaving the office. Dennis goes to pick up some letters he'd left on his secretary's desk, and discovers she hadn't gotten around to typing them yet. "No problem," he says with a forced smile. "Please have them done by ten tomorrow." As they drive home, Marc and Dennis are tired and thoughtful and exchange only a few words—a sharp contrast to their usually animated conversations.

Marc's wife Sara hears the business report on the radio while she fixes dinner. She has a good idea that Marc will come home exhausted and depressed, so she opens a bottle of his favorite wine. Marc walks in. He notices the wine and kisses Sara gently and gratefully on the back of her neck, then goes in the bathroom to wash up. During dinner, Marc talks a little about the day. Sara listens but doesn't push him for information. She knows he'll talk if he wants to, and that there are days when he'd rather keep it all in. Sara notices their youngest son is pushing food around on his plate instead of eating. Normally she might say something, but today she decides that since the boy isn't going to starve to death, there's no point making an issue of it when Marc is already tense.

After Dennis drops Marc off, he heads home. Timmy's bike is lying in the middle of the driveway again—"I'm gonna kill that kid," Dennis mutters to himself. One black thought piles on top of another: Marge can see the driveway through the kitchen window. You'd think she'd have the sense to get Timmy to put the bike away so I wouldn't have to stop the car and waste all this time. But no, she leaves all the discipline to me. It's a wonder she even wipes the kids' noses when they have a cold—she never notices anyone's needs besides her own.

Dennis enters the kitchen to find dinner's not ready yet. "Okay, okay," he says to his wife. "I'm going to lie down. At least *try* to keep the kids quiet, will you?"

"Fine," Marge says tightly; she stirs the soup so hard it some of it spills on the stove. Meanwhile she's thinking, I've been with the kids all day. For God's sake, you'd think their father would come home and want to spend a little time with them.

Man is probably the most aggressive species on earth. It takes a constant effort for two people to express tenderness toward each other; aggression sets in without our being aware of it.

Marc and Dennis are perfect examples of this concept. When Dennis discovered his secretary hadn't typed his letters, he wanted to explode. Dennis can't afford to get angry at his secretary any more than he could afford to get angry at all those customers who'd been calling all day. So he swallows his anger, then takes his aggression out on his wife and child.

Marc and Sara are under pressure, too, but they have agreed to make a conscious effort to be kind to each other. Granted, if Marc had come in slamming the door and screaming about dinner being late, it certainly would have been harder for Sara to make that effort. But Sara knows that today it's her turn to smooth her partner's path; tomorrow or the day after, should her day go awry, Mark will return the favor for her.

Marc and Sara have learned that if they do what's natural, they'll fight with each other. Again, tenderness doesn't come naturally, it requires conscious choice.

But in bonding together, Marc and Sara joined forces. They're aggressive together in the same way that they're dependent together. Instead of turning on each other, they unite their anger and direct it outward. Certainly there's enough happening in the world around them to justify that anger. And the fact that they don't have to be angry alone greatly reinforces their bond. As I pointed out at the start of this chapter, before people can successfully pair off, they've got to be mature enough to tolerate ambivalence. The longer they're together, the more they're going to become aware of each other's shortcomings. Successfully directing their aggression outward permits them to be more tolerant of each other. And the knowledge that they can trust their commitment permits them to be honest with each other.

AGGRESSION IS HALF OF US

If we trace the word *aggression* back to its Latin roots, we find one meaning is to *move toward*. I like that idea, because I know aggression is a necessary part of our lives. I feel that being aware of their aggression enables partners to move toward a mature relationship.

One of the worst things people can do is to deny their innate aggression. When I spoke about Gail, my friend who was mugged in Chicago, my point was that people who try to deny the aggressive tendencies in themselves and others, who envision a perfect world, expose themselves to needless danger. Aggression can be a wonderful thing. It helps us survive by enabling us to seek food and shelter. It helps preserve our self-esteem by preventing us from regressing to the point where we let someone else provide for all our needs. Most people who can't sustain a relationship deny the role of aggression in themselves and others.

The same energies that propelled us to leave our first idealized dependent relationship with Mother also assist us in discovering a new, mature, codependent relationship. Aggression allows us to keep growing and developing throughout adult relationships. Like infancy, the honeymoon doesn't last forever. As a new couple we feel secure, safe, insulated from the world. But then we must face life's realities. *Falling* in love must become *remaining* in love. Both partners must aggressively take 100 percent responsibility for the happiness and success of their commitments, including respect for the other's aggression.

Aggression can be a valued and trusted servant. For people whose personalities are well-developed and stable, a good part of aggression is monitored internally by conscience; they stop and think before they do something that may be momentarily pleasurable or expedient, but which will threaten the qualities of their relationship needs. But in those people with low self-esteem, aggression can step in and take over their lives. For them, aggression becomes destructive impulsivity.

6

Mission Impossible

If you've learned to appreciate the need for both dependency and aggression within yourself, then you're going to value these qualities in your mate as well. But if you're trying to ignore these needs in yourself, then you're going to attempt to ignore them in other people. You won't see your mate for what he is; instead, you're going to idealize him. And of course he's not going to be able to live up to your ideals. That's when the trouble starts.

Dreaming, idolizing another person, putting people up on a pedestal—all of these actions have a common objective: They help the dreamer, the idolizer, the pedestal-builder to avoid facing reality. Idealizing the other person always hearkens back to the concept of fusion—the idea that Mother and Child are one, or that Lover and Loved are one. Instead of growing individually and together, the two people involved cease to be committed to the responsibility of a relation. The fusion into one idealized being paradoxically leads us to become two selves; all the good is seen as "ours" while all the bad is either denied or "theirs." Sooner or later the good self will become determined to destroy the bad self; there's going to be a war.

Why is a war inevitable? To answer, let me get technical for a moment....

PERSONAL BEST

Psychoanalytic literature describes three elements that make up the personality.

First is the *id:* our instincts, our primitive drives. The id is impulsive, always trying to steer us toward what will be pleasurable.

Second is the *ego,* which attempts to integrate our perception and memory with our learned responses to the world around us. The ego bases itself in the real world and allows us to cope with reality to avoid pain as best as possible.

Third is the *superego,* composed of two parts: the *ego-ideal,* which is essentially the striving to be special in the eyes of others, and the *conscience,* which is our internalized conceptions of good and bad. This superego is the part of us that makes us strive for perfection and is thus of most concern to us as we explore the problem of codependency.

There are many ways that parents who overvalue their children can give them a false impression of who they are. For example, all three- and four-year-olds want to be the main object of their parents' attention. Some children think they must attract attention by being exactly what Mommy or Daddy expect. The belief that our value is derived from pleasing the others has early roots. Naturally those kids will become frustrated when they learn they *can't* do it all—at least not yet. Growing up means accepting limits, having realistic ego ideals, and facing the reality that they're not always their parents' main focus.

The best parents are the ones who successfully convey that each child is unique and that they love that child for what he or she is. On the other hand, if a child's stock with his parents rises and falls with his performance—if they love him for what he *does,* rather than what he *is*—that child will grow up with a very distorted sense of reality. He will devote all his psychic energies to pretending, lying, or creating some complicated world in which he will always be Number One—what we call being narcisstic.

When a mother loves her child for what he is, he internalizes that love and, as a result, has less need for external approval from his spouse. If the mother loves a child only for what he accomplishes, then he must continually reinforce his sense of self-esteem by deeds and being noticed. Similarly, people need to appreciate their mates for who they are, not for what they do in the relationship. Accepting their mates' individuality—recognizing and embracing the differences between them—is essential if the two partners hope to continue to desire each other.

The young adolescent loves himself. So does the adult who becomes stuck in pregenital infatuations. He picks a person out of the crowd and begins a relationship. At first he appears to idealize the other person, but in reality he is doing nothing more than building up his own sense of self-esteem. He is trying to be his own ideal, just as he was in infancy. He doesn't see the other person for what she really is; instead he loves her for what he wants her to be. In short, her being perfect will make up for his own faults. The purpose of the relationship is for him to look good.

PERFECTION PERSONIFIED

For the adult with an extremely demanding superego, nothing less than perfection will suffice. Such a person is the ultimate Ruler. Virtue is more important to him than truth.

My friend Jack is one of those people who's always in the middle of things. He took over his father's business ten years ago, and he's tripled its value. Now he's president of the Rotary, active in the church and the Big Brothers, and can always be relied on to help out a friend. Sometimes there's a little voice inside him telling him he'd better slow down, he's headed straight for a heart attack, but he doesn't pay any attention. He's frankly afraid to slow down. If he isn't working on a hundred projects at once, he might have to face himself, and he's terrified that "self" won't live up to his own expectations. Perhaps not surprisingly, Jack has never married. He's had a lot of passionate involvements, but the moment a woman reveals the slightest hint of an "imperfection" he rejects her.

THE UNDESERVING

Robin, a 30-year-old word processor: "Here's my pattern with friendships. I've been doing this ever since grade school. I find a guy I like. I start building him up to myself. I think about how wonderful he is—cute, funny, talented, caring—while at the same time I'm trying to win him over as a friend. Then finally we become friends—and all of a sudden I no longer value him. I mean, if he was willing to be close with me, he couldn't be much good, could he? It's like that Groucho Marx joke—I wouldn't belong to a club that would have me for a member. I guess I thought falling in love would be different. I thought if a guy could really love me I'd finally be able to respect both him and myself. I should have known better."

Clark, on the other hand, is one of those guys who's not going to let anything shatter his love-ideal, no matter what it costs him. The moment his current woman begins to slip from her pedestal, Clark runs off. Rather than deal with reality by accepting the inevitable problems and make an effort to keep the relationship going, he'll find someone else. Maybe if he'd face reality, his friends keep telling him, he'd be able to stay with a woman for more than six months. But it's no use talking to him. "I could see it coming," he'll tell his friends. "Anne (or Betty or Carolyn or Dana) is so wonderful, but I could see we were starting to argue more and more of the time. If I stayed around any longer, I'd only drag her down, and she doesn't deserve that. She shouldn't waste any more of her valuable time—she's too good for a guy like me."

The pursuit of perfect, idealized love leads only to disappointment—how can it not? That grail doesn't exist. The search for such a mythical love only serves to reactivate all the insecurities you felt as a toddler. And since you can't "repair" an illusion, there's no way to ultimately feel good about yourself. People like Robin and Clark at first appear extremely masochistic: They seem to act in ways that hurt only themselves. On closer look, however, we see their narcissistic personalities as well. A caring relationship will expose their dire need to be admired from external sources because of their internal emptiness.

THE IDOL MAKERS

There are three different forms of idealization. In its most infantile form, a person divides everything into black or white, bad or good. If a loved one slips from the pedestal, he or she must be punished. For as long as the person chooses to see the loved one as "all good," any of their failings will be ignored. This is the level at which most people with sick personalities are stuck.

At a second, more familiar level, we may become aware of a person's shortcomings, but are so anxious to idealize the person that we turn these liabilities into assets. "Poor Rick," Leda said, "he's had such an unhappy life. Let me tell you, if you had a family like his, you'd drown your sorrows in drink too. The only reason he drinks so much is because he's so sensitive and he's in pain. He wants to help his parents but he sees how hopeless it is...." This second level of idealization—demonstrated in this case as the ability to transform alcoholism into a virtue—is typical of most neurotic people. At root, however, the neurotic person expects a reward for her love: "I stood by you and defended you when people called you a lush! You owe me a lot, buster!"

The third level of idealization, which many healthy people experience as young adults, is when we can pretty much see people realistically for what they are but we still tend to idealize them. Take Mike and Joan, for example. They met during the sixties, on a bus headed for a civil rights march. They sat together, got talking, and discovered their views to be extremely complementary. Having been raised in the South, Joan wasn't as gung-ho about civil rights as other people Mike knew. Mike valued that. Also, the more they talked, the more Mike got the sense that she still loved and respected her parents, even though they held many bigoted views. Too many people he knew had gotten angry and broken away from home because they disagreed with their parents' political viewpoints. But Joan really seemed to be able to keep everything in perspective. So did Mike and Joan throughout their relationship—their shared ideals drew them together, but after their initial meeting, they continued dating and found they continued to enjoy each others' presence.

DENNIS AND MARGE AGAIN

Remember Dennis and Marge, whom we met in Chapter Five. The fact that their marriage is on a downhill course is fairly obvious. And yet when they married nine years ago, they were both good, well-intentioned people. It really looked like they could make a go of it.

Marge was one of five children. Although her father worked hard, the family was never able to make ends meet. But she was determined to get an education and to "marry up" in the world. She worked as a secretary during the day, went to the local university at night. Then she met Dennis, a fast-rising stockbroker. He was everything her father wasn't—clean-cut, well-educated, a go-getter. At the tender age of 25, the amount he paid just in income taxes was twice as high as what her father earned in a year. Here, finally, was a man Marge felt she could respect.

They married and bought a home that cost over $200,000. They joined the country club; Dennis said it was a good place to meet potential clients. Marge dropped out of school and quit her job. Because Dennis said he was eager to throw dinner parties, Marge took a course in gourmet cooking. Then she began having children, children who would be going to the best private schools in the area. What more could she have asked for?

Well, she could have asked for Dennis to be home more. She wanted a man who would work hard, but not *that* hard. Her father might not have had much money to spend, but at least he spent time with his children. And Dennis was so tense all the time, he'd throw a fit if the kids were crying or if he found a spot on the carpet.

THE EVE OF DESTRUCTION

In the beginning of their relationship, Marge focused on how wonderful Dennis was: how different he was from her father, how capable he was at making money, how aggressive he was in his work. She looked at the tangible evidence that things were good: She had the expensive house she'd always wanted. Her children had their every need provided for—*they'll* never have to wear discarded clothes like I did, she told herself. But she wasn't being honest about what she wanted, and why she wanted it.

Marge told herself she respected Dennis. But the word respect, in Latin, means "to look back." Marge had never looked back carefully at the man she'd married or the course of their lives together. If she had, she would have realized that their relationship didn't become destructive overnight but instead had been problematic from the start. For the first few years they were married, they went out of their way to be kind to each other. They both insisted they had an ideal marriage; neither would admit that the other had any flaws. Instead of observing the differences between them and loving each other in spite of them, they simply pretended the differences weren't there.

Most marriage counselors will tell you that it takes about

seven years for the destructiveness to show up in a relationship. Dennis would probably disagree; he feels the destruction began to set in around the time the kids were born, four years after his marriage. At that time Marge seemed to change. She was no longer able to manage on her own, so he hired a full-time maid in an effort to help. But it wasn't that Marge was too busy; she just didn't seem able to make decisions on her own. Even simple things like choosing what to make for dinner threw her for a loop. Dennis thought, Maybe I should try to be around more. He took a little time off, only to hear Marge complain that he was "always underfoot, just like the kids."

The more he tried to do for her, the less she seemed to appreciate him. She began to take offense at everything he said, no matter how innocent. He had to choose his words carefully, to make sure he didn't offend her. But the more he tried to hold himself in check, the more he found himself exploding in anger. As a result, he went in the opposite direction and began spending more time at the office. At least it was quiet there. What Dennis failed to see, of course, was that he was reacting to *her* reactions to *him*. He was just as much a participant as she was in a never-ending cycle.

MARGE HERSELF

Marge's marriage had problems because Marge had problems. Her personality had some serious defects. All her behavior was organized around self-defense. Marge had never gotten over her anger at her father—for not making enough money, but also for not loving her as much as he loved her mother. Unless something changed, Marge would never be able to love someone in a healthy and positive way, and make that love last forever, no matter how much she might have wanted to.

At the beginning of their marriage she felt cherished and special. But the moment she sensed that Dennis no longer worshiped her in the same way he did on their honeymoon, a thought formed in her head: He was just like her father. He was never going to love her as much as she wanted, so she stopped wanting *any* love. Because she'd never developed the ability to make reparation, or to trust her own goodness, she was unable to tolerate frustration. All she could do was make Dennis feel guilty—and she got very good at doing *that*.

A newborn baby does not know how to *give* love, only

how to take it. Naturally, we don't expect an infant to respect the fact that Mommy hasn't slept in three nights because he's been up crying. In his mind, Mommy only counts when she comes to feed and hold him. When we look at deteriorating adult relationships, we see similar interactions. Even when they were first married, Marge seldom stopped to consider what Dennis wanted. She was more concerned with what she wanted from him. The only time she did think about it was when she was angry. At such moments she would think to herself, He wants a cook, not a wife, or, He's ashamed to come with me when I visit my parents.

Eventually the problems Marge brought to her marriage became the couple's problems. Marge didn't trust her own strengths, and nothing Dennis could do would have helped that. She was angry at herself for never being good enough. But, she would think, what am I supposed to do, kill myself? Of course not. She found it was easier to think of herself as trying so hard, or to see it as all her father's fault, or her husband's fault. In doing so, Marge was using one of the most common of all human psychological defense mechanisms: projection. Projecting means attributing our own fears and anger to other people, and usually we project onto the people we're closest with. Although it's not really possible to simply stop doing so, we *can* try to be more aware of our projections, and to understand the needs that motivate them.

BACK TO BASICS

Relationships don't just "fail." Most of them have been destroyed. Think about Marge and Dennis when they were first married—how she insisted he was perfect. She was idealizing him. But *at its most primitive level, idealization conceals hate.* In other words, if you have to make such a show of love, then you're probably trying to convince yourself that love exists where in reality it is absent. Take a closer look at any couple you know that's been unable to sustain a relationship, and you'll probably see the seeds of destruction were planted on Day One.

7

"Making" Love

In 1987, when the movie *Fatal Attraction* came out, I had recently launched the codependency program at NorthShore Psychiatric Hospital. In the movie Dan, the character played by Michael Douglas, is a young executive whose wife and daughter are away for the weekend. He meets Alex (Glenn Close) at a business meeting, and spends the weekend in bed with her. She refuses to accept that their relationship was only a weekend affair. She chases after him and becomes increasingly destructive when he doesn't respond to her advances. Finally she grabs a butcher knife and goes after Dan's wife, who manages to kill Alex.

I thought quite a lot about all the havoc this twisted relationship had caused in "Dan's" life. I thought I'd develop a lecture around that movie, creating alternative scenarios to illustrate all the obstacles codependents face as they attempt recovery. For example, if Dan hadn't already been married, he might have married Alex. In that case I suspected that their marriage would have been similar to Marge and Dennis' (see Chapter Five.) That first weekend, I'm sure Alex thought she wanted everything Marge wanted—the beautiful home on Long Island, the angelic children. It was going to be ideal. Maybe her destructive tendencies would have been toned down somewhat, given the relative security of the marriage. But although it certainly would have taken longer for those tendencies to come out, they would have been there, lying dormant, waiting to erupt.

The more I looked, the more problems I began to see with this fable of the poor innocent man who ends up in a destructive relationship. I realized that Dan had a lot of personal difficulties even before he met Alex. If he'd been more psychologically stable himself, he'd have never become so caught up in her eroticism. If he had been more clear-headed, he could never have ignored the signals that warned how sick she was. Instead, he deluded himself into thinking he'd met an exciting woman. The sexual aspects of the relationship would continue to dominate the first few years of their marriage, disguising the underlying difficulties the couple was having. Then suddenly, when the bloom is off the sexual rose, their seemingly happy life would blow up in their faces.

Emphasizing sexuality is a universal and seemingly easy technique people use to idealize, and thus obscure, a destructive relationship. Many people who come to me for help report that they have used a wide variety of sexual strategies—multiple positions, multiple orgasms, sexual toys, X-rated movies—to try to "fix" their failing relationships. But the same people who idealize the sexual aspects are usually the ones with severe personality impairments. It's difficult, if not impossible, for them to sustain a mature relationship. So they take what they can get.

PIPE DREAMS: THE SIXTIES REVISITED

As I recall, the 1950s were a pretty scary time in America. I graduated high school then. What I remember most vividly were all the bomb shelters and air raid drills. People thought the world was going to end any day; for many, life was losing a great deal of its meaning. That attitude was reflected every-where, from Cold War politics to popular culture. People seemed to say, for example, why listen to classical music—so long and complicated? Why not listen to Elvis, instead—short, punchy songs? Let's be chaotic. Let's all love each other, let's all feel good, because we might all be gone tomorrow. In a weird way, by dwelling on thoughts about the bomb, we started acting as if the bomb had already fallen. I wonder how many potentially rewarding relationships were to be ruined by this kind of thinking.

As a kind of backlash from the fearful worries of the fifties, the sixties erupted in color, light, and sound. There were the Flower Children, psychedelic drugs, outrageous music. Everything was loving and peaceful—or so the utopian vision would have us believe. Due in part to our involvement in Vietnam, aggression was seen as a vile and evil thing. Instead, went the philosophy of the day, all you need is love. But the downside of this philosophy was kept under wraps. The dangerous aspects of free love were largely denied. People seldom mentioned such things as sexually transmitted diseases back in those days. Today, in the Age of AIDS, it's a little harder to deny the dangers of free sex.

We inhabitants of the 1990s look back smugly on these past eras and think to ourselves, How naive those poor people were then. How sophisticated we are today. Perhaps. But many people in the current age still fall prey to utopian thinking and misguided idealism.

Take the animal rights activists, for example. They march out in front of the medical school with placards that say "Don't do research on animals." I would ask, "What about the *people* who are going to die because we weren't able to discover and test new medications? Shouldn't we protect them, too?" The activists shrug; they seem unable to see both the good and bad. The acceptance of differences and compromise seems threatening to them.

If you ask any of these people about their aggressions, they'll look at you as if you're crazy. They're talking about ideal worlds, and you're telling them that they have aggressions? Forget it! Aggression is bad—it's war, murder, violence. Killing animals is sadistic aggression. If we stop doing such horrible things, aggression won't exist. (Here we see the denial system.)

But as I've been saying all along, *aggression is half of our makeup*. It is a vital part of nature. Refusing to acknowledge it is like refusing to recognize a truck that's about to run you over. If you don't concentrate on channeling aggression in constructive ways, then it will overpower you. *We have got to pay attention to reality*. We can't let ourselves idealize things so much that we ignore the troublesome aspects of life. By idealizing, people try to hide their public displays of aggression and anger. The more they do that, the more their anger must be directed at their mates or their children—all the people closest to them.

One of the catch phrases that emerged in the sixties was "do your own thing." I like to imagine stepping into a time machine, popping up in a hippie commune circa 1967, and trying to tell people about the human need for dependent relationships—not "do your own thing" but "do *our* own thing." I would explain how healthy people begin by having codependency with the mother in infancy and grow into adult relationships with an equal partner which take into account the need for shared dependency and shared aggression. I suspect if I did, however, I'd be laughed out of the room, or the tent, or wherever. The emphasis in the sixties was on self-satisfaction (if it feels good, do it), and that's the same concept my patients tell me they see touted today in much of the literature on codependency. Self-satisfaction is fine, up to a point. But what self-satisfied people ignore is the fact that most humans are at their best when they're comfortable with dependency.

THE JOY OF SEXUALITY

People proclaimed the sixties as a time of sexual revolution. Every illicit drug that appeared was praised for its aphrodisiac qualities. Having great sex was considered more important than having a sustained relationship of which sex was but one element. A vestige of this sexual utopia can be seen today in the "open marriage," where partners agree to have as many affairs as they wish. But equating sex and love proved to be an empty exercise. As many people discovered to their chagrin, when sexual satisfaction is the goal, sexual happiness is rare.

We have to look at our sexual needs in the same way we look at our needs for dependency and aggression. Sexuality can either be an asset or a liability, depending upon what we do with it. The choice is up to us. As we saw in Chapter 4, only after the genital component enters a relationship can we truly speak of "love." Once introduced, this sexual element remains a constant aspect of all love relations, setting into play a fluctuating cycle of fear, reparation, and shared growth. As I explained, by sexual I don't mean gymnastic feats performed in the arena of the bedroom. It means transforming individual needs into mutual pleasures. The female with her mutually valued vagina is complemented by the male and his mutually valued penis.

As you no doubt realize, sex—genital, orgasmic sex—is a great way to release built-up tension. In fact, intercourse is in many ways a process of *creating* tension for the pure pleasure of having it relieved. But remember our earlier discussion of sexuality, which involves not just physical contact but emotional contact as well. Sexual desire can also produce a healthy and energizing tension, but in the best relationships that energy can be released in the form of tenderness or affection. Healthy relationships combine genital and nongenital love. That's why I strongly object to the way we use the phrase "making love." We need to keep aware that love can also mean taking a walk, watching a movie, going for a ride, working around the house, or sitting in the living room reading. Intercourse is a lovely part of the picture—but only a part. When we limit "making love" to sexual intercourse alone, we're ignoring the importance of respecting and valuing each other as whole individuals.

TRANSCENDENCE, NOT FUSION

Take a normal healthy couple on a Saturday night. They've had a relaxing day, maybe they went out for dinner, now they come home and go to bed. They begin by gently cuddling each other's bodies—hands, arms, the back of the neck, the soft swell of the cheek. That action stirs up feelings that connect them subconsciously to the pleasure they felt being cuddled in their mother's arms long ago. At some point the genitals come into play. Finally they join together in a way that goes beyond anything the infant and the mother could ever achieve; they become one flesh through sexual union.

Recall that fusion with the mother's body took place when the infant had no awareness that he and his mother were separate beings. But as adults we are fully aware that we and our partners are discrete beings. We recognize our anatomical differences—we thrive on them—and ideally we desire not just our partner's body but the mind and soul as well. We also realize that at best this desire is mutual. Somewhere in our minds is the notion that, if it were ever articulated, would sound something like this: "It's essential to me that my lover desires and needs my body as much as I desire and need hers. That feeling helps me overcome the frustration I experienced as an infant, when I needed my mother's body but I knew she never needed mine." The experience of mutual need can carry us to an exciting, gratifying state of bliss, often culminating in shared orgasm. Within such bliss, sometimes aided by conscious or unconscious fantasy, we experience true contentment and the illusion of fulfillment. But this experience of wholeness is momentary at best.

Dr. Kernberg has said that "the most important boundaries crossed in sexual passion are those of the self." In other words, a person might think, I want to merge with another, I want to experience our oneness. Let me speak personally for a moment. As a man, I want to grow beyond masculinity; I want to know what femininity means, what it feels like. During intercourse I cross the boundary that separates our two bodies, I experience that final mystery of the feminine to the largest possible degree for me. I momentarily *transcend myself* in an experience that can be described not just in physical but in spiritual terms. I speak only for myself as a man here; ideally, if the desire for each other's body is mutual, then my wife experiences a similar sense of fulfillment.

But I also experience the pleasure of pure genital stimulation as well. In the psychoanalytic way of thinking, this stimulation recalls and fulfills the early homosexual urges I felt toward my father. As a child I felt a subconscious envy toward my father's ability to possess my mother; I envied them together in their bedroom at night. Now, as an adult, I'm finally able to relate to the woman I love in the way my father related to my mother. I loved my father deeply all the while I was competing with him, so I don't feel destructive toward my partner; all I want to do is unite with her. I shudder to think what it might have been like if I hadn't loved my father, I'd most likely be acting like Don Juan, being unable to respect women or myself. Fortunately, my father's relationship with both my mother and me taught me to appreciate tenderness. Here, I am emphasizing what I often call *prerequisite love*. The son's acceptance of his father's love, and the daughter's acceptance of the mother's love are an important and often complex preparation to heterosexual love.

When sexual fusion has ended, and I'm outside my partner's body once again, the world looks slightly different. Everything around me takes on more meaning. Having truly identified with another person, I have a better understanding of who I am, while my longing for her continues.

Being drawn back to reality is the inevitable consequence of experiencing passion. "Passion" comes from the Greek word *pathos,* which means to suffer or endure. In past eras, the word was used to describe martyrdom. Today we use passion to

ONE-WAY DESIRE

It's extremely important to me that my wife desire my body as much as I desire hers. To me this seems the most natural thing in the world. But for people with unhealthy personalities, such mutual desire can be extremely threatening.

Consider the case of Arlene. Arlene claims she doesn't need sexual gratification for herself. All that matters to her is that her lovers achieve orgasm. "Just watching my lover's happiness at that moment is pleasure enough for me," she says.

But Arlene will also admit, when questioned, that most of the lovers she chooses are "broken people." By that she means that they are psychologically *incapable* of reciprocating the pleasure she's giving them. Arlene finds their relations pleasurable only so long as she thinks she is easing their troubles, repairing the damage done to them in the past.

The problem is that sometimes her "repairs" are too effective. When she has satisfied her lovers and they begin to focus their efforts on giving *her* pleasure, Arlene panics. She tightens up and feels stagnant inside. She feels afraid that she will lose control. Of course, in a very real sense, that's the whole point of sexual intercourse. But somewhere in her mind Arlene transforms the loss of control into a feeling that she will somehow hurt her lover (with her denied hostilities). Whenever a lover triggers such feelings, Arlene feels compelled to abandon the relationship. She runs away, emotionally and physically.

Paula has a different strategy for avoiding mutual desire: She makes sure to keep her desires on what she calls a "short leash." She and Carl have worked together for three years now, and she's loved him from the start. But Paula "knows" how ugly she is. She tells herself that if Carl ever saw her naked he'd run screaming in the other direction. She might spend half the day fantasizing about going to bed with him, but she believes that if she ever lets on she's interested, he'll reject her. She imagines she'd be so embarrassed she'd quit her job. As long as Paula keeps playing this broken record in her head—"I must keep my distance"—the self-fulfilling prophecy will come true.

mean any strong emotion, including affection or hatred, as well as intense sexual desire. Passion thus refers to a whole spectrum of experiences: the desire to be transformed, the pleasure or anguish of that transformation, the return to reality, and the longing to transcend once more. Whenever two people successfully integrate their passions—their aggressions and dependencies, their need for each other, to desire as much as they wish to be desired—mature love is possible. When disguised, hidden, or unreciprocated, passion becomes a dark and dangerous force.

BEING OBJECTIVE

Mutual respect comes before mutual desire. As we saw in previous chapters, respect implies the ability to tolerate ambivalence. Before a person can identify with his own sexuality and that of his partner, he must mentally integrate love and hate into the unified feeling I will call concern. During infancy—the preverbal stage of life—passion dominates the scene. In a sense, babies are pure emotion. But the experiences of life and growth during childhood tame and socialize that primal passion. When as adults we have intercourse, the passion we feel makes us feel infantile, vulnerable, and extremely dependent once again. We must consciously choose to activate our aggressive instincts through this kind of physical and emotional excitement if we want our relationships to remain stable.

Some couples enjoy playfully "exploiting" each other as part of their sexual games. They temporarily regress into "good" and "bad" selves. At its core, this aggression (it is, in fact, a mild form of masochism) fuels the couple's mutual passions and increases their continued fascination and their ability to bond with each other. At a more intense level of masochism, however, that process is reversed; eroticism fuels aggression. In any case, if the partners hope to enjoy such sex play, if they hope to enjoy sex without any threat to their pleasure, they must each come to terms with their own needs for dependency and aggression. In the process of being and growing together, the couple defines these concepts on their own terms. For example, to a masochist aggression will mean something different than to other people. Defining these terms in a clear and mutually agreeable way is by no means an easy task.

SEX OBJECTS

Sexual desire, often the basis of our first attraction to another person, is always an attraction to an object. The sex object remains just that—an object, not a person. When sexual impulses motivate us, we tend to ignore the other person's human attributes; we suppress our ability to see good and bad. We even lose sight of those qualities that make the individual we desire different from other people and focus instead on our desire for instant pleasure and gratification. At this level, sex with one object is the same as with the next. People trapped in this mode of thinking often move from object to object. When men or women are still stuck at a primitive level of development— if they still cling to those transitional objects that they used as replacements for the incestual bond—then they will tend to use each lover as a temporary object. Clearly, their sense of self hasn't progressed very far from when they were three years old. Because the "object" they desire is actually the mother, no sexual relationship, no matter how spirited, will be very rewarding.

Some people caught up in this cycle take great pride in conquering, and then discarding, one "object" after another. Other people, such as the woman who falls for the drug addict who obviously can't return her love, are unknowingly keeping the incestual object out of harm's way. Or, in still another scenario, the woman chooses the man who will abuse her, thus feeling duly punished for attempting to find a replacement for her mother's love.

Any lover who wants to keep his beloved under control assumes he can possess her fully. He cannot bear to face reality, he can't stand the thought of the other person's separate existence. He's going to have to look his lover in the face and realize she's not what he first desired. He's got no choice but to turn her into an object.

In Chapter Two, we saw how the child who is attempting to separate from its mother will take possession of one object after another, using the objects to help make the transition to greater independence. As a psychiatrist, when I work with patients to examine how their relationships have failed, we are actually studying how well, or how poorly, the individual achieved that first separation. What is perhaps the most hopeful sign in many of these people is that they have other, stable friendships. So long as a friendship does not involve sexual elements, they usually are able to tolerate ambivalence. The inability to maintain lasting friendships is clearly a pessimistic sign for lasting sexual relationships. On a day-to-day level, the couple's relationship reflects mutual concern and commitment. But keep in mind that friendships are much easier than love relationships. Just about all a friendship requires is acceptance, whereas lasting love requires giving, receiving, and passion.

"GOOD" OR "BAD"?

Meet Frances, a sixty-year-old woman who has always lived alone and who is extremely successful in a cosmetics business she started nearly thirty-five years ago. Think she's independent? Take a closer look. Frances is incapable of being either dependent or aggressive with a person she loves. The same holds true for Max, that gorgeous man, the one with the great job, a three-piece suit, and just the right amount of gray in his hair. Max is the type who is likely to leave his wife when he turns fifty and marry his secretary, because she "minds him" and does everything he asks without complaining. Sex isn't an intimate experience for Max. Oh, sure, it's proof that he's still young, that he can still "be a man." But he's spent most of his life performing for his mother, and still he's got to have her undivided attention.

Is crying good or bad? Is being a perfectionist good or bad? Everything rests upon our mature acceptance of the needs for dependency and aggression. A woman's femininity does not depend upon long flowing hair or big breasts, no matter what image the glamour magazines might try to convey. Nor can we define masculinity as a hairy chest and firm muscles, a love for sports cars, a collection of girlie magazines, or the number of notches on the sexual belt. What defines masculinity and femininity—our gender identity—is our ability to love and to sustain that love. The benchmark of mental health, against which we measure everything, is a person's ability to subordinate the primary interest in the self and form an enduring relationship with a person of the opposite sex.

THE PRIMROSE PATH

We have to redefine what we mean by making love. The couple who shares respect and commitment does not *have* to perform wondrous feats in bed in order to express their mutual sexuality. In contrast, couples who idealize each other's sexuality without taking a look at the whole person are headed for trouble. I always tell the interns and residents I've worked with: "When patients come to you and say they have a sex problem, they're trying to lead you down the primrose path. To find the clues to their problems, look elsewhere." By that remark I mean that such patients want easy answers in support of their denial system. They are trying to cast the doctor in the role of parent, so the "parent" can then give them permission to become sexually involved with an Oedipal substitute. This strategy might alleviate the symptoms for a brief period, but I guarantee it won't last.

Sex itself is a very simple thing; we humans are the ones who make it complicated. Most sexual problems occur when a couple's aggressiveness isn't balance by tenderness. Woman after woman comes into my office in tears. All of the sudden her marriage has gone to hell. She doesn't know what happened, she just woke up one day and found she'd lost sexual interest in her husband. Well, my guess is that the "interest" was missing from the start, and to disguise that fact the couple directed all of their attention toward physical gratification. The truth is, physical gratification may be the first thing to go when the fundamental relationship is failing.

REAL NEEDS

When people can't successfully reconcile their needs for dependency and aggression, their sexual fantasies—and often their sexual behavior itself—will be saturated with hostility. George, a patient who came to see me recently, is a perfect example. In his sexual fantasies, he's always sexually entering his partner from behind. "I get excited fast that way," he explains. "I can't stand it when a partner looks me in the eyes. I can't help thinking I'm going to burst out crying," he finally admits. George needs to be in control; he'll conceal his need for dependency by degrading his partner. In this case, degradation means avoiding eye contact and having anal desires.

Humans, supposedly the crown of creation, are the only creatures who usually have intercourse face to face. The person with personality development problems cannot take pleasure in simple genital intercourse and shared orgasm. Instead such people do something to dramatize (spoil) that special moment, because they don't want to admit that their own bodies don't contain everything they need. They idealize the sex act itself. They create their own definition of "pleasure"; to a greater or lesser extent it's a perverted pleasure.

Such people will alternately cling to their lovers and then push them away. For them, physical sex will involve degrading the partner. But as the relationship ages, then suddenly it is no longer a fantasy but a mundane reality; at that point one partner becomes bored, or starts to find the other repulsive. Hatred sets in, not because the sex life fails but because the person is struggling too hard to maintain independence.

When people idealize their partners, or the sex act itself, they deny their feelings of hatred. They have to, otherwise they would lose their partners forever. My patients tell me that the books on codependency all talk about denial. From what I've seen, however, these books describe codependents as denying something that lies outside of themselves: "Person A denied her husband's abusiveness," or "Patient B tried to deny her boyfriend drank as much as he did." Such books miss the point. What codependents have *really* been denying all this time is *their own aggressive nature*.

Some so-called experts claim that the codependent's need *for* love is the problem. In truth, the problem is that the codependent is unable to *give* love. She's still locked in her childish demands of wanting to be given love by the parent (and parent substitute); she has convinced herself that receiving that love is a matter of life or death. The mature adult, through shared genital sex and orgasm, learns that giving is an essential part of pleasure. But the codependent can't reach this level, because she's unable to mobilize her aggression in the constructive service of passion.

You've heard it said that there is "safety in numbers." When they become sexually bored, many people have affairs hoping that renewing their interest in sex with another person will renew their interest in their spouse as well. But promiscuity denies dependency. If the couple openly agrees to extramarital affairs, they don't feel as guilty about using one man or woman to replace the beloved parent. We're right back to the false promises of the sixties again. But creating utopias isn't the answer now any more than it was a generation ago. There's still a person behind all these "problems" and that person's still stuck in some early phase of development that's interfering with his or her capacity to sustain a loving relationship.

8

When Idols Fall

One day a new patient joins our therapy group. I introduce Martin and ask him to say a few words about himself and why he is here. "Well, I'm thirty-six years old, a manager for a video rental store," he says. "I've been married for fourteen years. But I've been having affairs for over twelve years now."

Although the others in the group try not to show any reactions, I can sense a growing tension in the air. "You have to understand," Martin says. "My wife and I have—well, I guess you could call it an understanding. The first couple of years after we were married I tried to keep my relationships with other women a secret. But ten years ago my wife found out what was going on. We've been fairly open about it ever since. I knew she wasn't too thrilled about it, but she knows I love her and the kids and I work hard to provide for them, so she's put up with it.

"Recently, though, the marriage began falling apart. I thought she understood I had needs outside the marriage. Except for those first two years, I thought being open about everything was the best thing I could do. But something must have really been bothering her, something she couldn't bring herself to talk to me about. I never expected her to just pick up the kids and leave all of a sudden. That's what she did three months ago.

"I don't know where to turn now. I feel a little confused. So that's why I've decided to come in for therapy."

The others in the group listen quietly as Martin tells his story. I ask if anyone has any reactions. At first their remarks are polite and objective: They ask for more information, they clarify points. Soon, though, things take a turn. Subtly at first, then more brazenly, four women in the group begin challenging Martin. "Why don't you just go live with your current lover?" Deborah snaps.

Martin tries to explain: "My current lover's in college and lives in an apartment with two other girls. She's only twenty years old." When he admits that most of his affairs have been with much younger women, the women really get incensed.

"How could you do this to your wife?" one asks. "Don't you realize how awful she must feel?"

"How could you destroy your marriage this way?" demands another.

Martin is somewhat taken aback by their remarks. I can tell from his eyes that he expected something different from a group therapy session. But I have a reason for letting the discussion take its own course.

You see, what the women in the group are not yet willing to admit to Martin is that they too have been unable to maintain healthy monogamous relationships. Through their attitudes and behavior they caused their marriages to fall apart. The only difference between them and Martin is that their destruction has followed a different path.

MALE AND FEMALE ENDINGS

Having affairs is the classic—and simplest—way to destroy what's left of a marriage. If you look at any ten failing marriages, you're probably going to see nine men who are involved with other lovers—but probably no more than one or two women in the same boat, although we are lately seeing more and more promiscuous wives.

The gap in that statistic is the product of two main factors: innate female sexuality and the different experiences men and women have in their early development. Remember what we've learned about the common rivalry between the daughter and her mother. Through sexual union with her partner, a woman regains some of that long awaited fusion she gave up in separation from the mother. But that's only a part of the picture. If she becomes pregnant, she experiences attachment on another level, this time with her child. She endures nine months of pregnancy, she knows what it felt like to have the fetus gestating inside her body. Gestation teaches her patience.

This deeper understanding of a need for fusion and patience generally gives women a better grasp on monogamous commitments, allowing them to balance their ambivalent feelings and prevent acting adulterously. Even though a woman might feel unhappy in her marriage or angry at her partner, she's less likely to rush into an adulterous relationship. She will most often select other ways of expressing her anger and misery—ways which keep her from looking bad.

Her husband, on the other hand, is probably still competing psychologically with his father for the mother's love. The man often fears the same fusion, which the woman has patiently awaited. After all, the mother is female; if the boy seeks fusion with the mother, he risks his maleness. He lacks the ability to achieve attachment on as many levels as a woman can, but wishes he could. Such wishes, though, are based less on reality and more on fantasy. The more a man realizes this "reality gap," the more he feels himself losing control of a situation. Often in such cases the result is that he becomes sexually uninterested in his wife and becomes involved with another woman whom he *can* control. In my view, men more easily turn to promiscuity or the use of drugs or alcohol because such behavior serves as a "substitute" for intimacy with a woman they might admire—a woman like Mother.

In Chapter Three, we saw how the little boy who is loved too dearly by his mother is not threatened by the reality of a father and often develops an inflated sense of himself which in turn may lead to the development of a perverse sense of sexuality. Similarly, the little girl loved too dearly by her father becomes unsure of herself and is at risk of becoming neurotic. In one common form of behavior, a woman will automatically assume responsibility for destroying her marriage. As a result she may go into a deep depression or take an overdose of pills. Whatever the particulars, she turns her destructiveness against herself.

WHAT WOULD HAPPEN IF...

Now let's return to the group therapy session. Martin is in a corner, figuratively speaking, and is trying desperately to defend himself. I step in to point out that promiscuity is perhaps the quickest and most efficient way to destroy a relationship. But what, I ask, are some other ways?

I turn to Deborah. "Martin doesn't know yet that you attempted suicide twice," I remark. "Think for a moment about what you put your husband through. You were in effect saying, 'If you leave me I'll kill myself. You don't love me the way I want you to, so I'm going to take these pills.' Is that accurate?" Deborah nods.

"But your husband left anyway. He told you, in effect, that he couldn't be responsible for your actions, so he split. Is that any less painful or less effective a way of destroying a marriage than what Martin has told us about?" There was a long silence before Deborah responded, "No, I guess not."

The other women haven't gone as far as Deborah did when she attempted suicide, but most of them had been acting depressed for years. I ask them to imagine how their depression might have eroded their relationship. "What might it feel like," I ask. "Your husband comes home, he's smiling, he had a good day at work today or is hopeful regarding a promotion, and he kisses you and asks how your day was. All you can say is 'I'm depressed.' "

Depression is one of the most destructive things that can happen to an individual. It is a relentless mood that, if untreated, can destroy not just the person but her relationships as well. More women than our society likes to admit go through periods of depression when they discover that marriage doesn't seem to be everything they expected. Any time you idealize something, you're opening yourself up to becoming depressed. Depression can set in the moment you discover your idols— your spouse, your lover, your parents—have clay feet. All of a sudden you realize you have to surrender your dreams; "This isn't the perfect marriage!" you cry with dismay. "My husband doesn't love me as much as I expected! He is not the perfect mate I thought he was!" "I am trapped in misery"... Devaluing creates misery and depression.

"DO SOMETHING FOR ME!"

Ten-year-old Bobby is stuck in the house on a rainy day. He calls out to Mommy and says he's bored. He's saying, in effect, "Do something for me! Play a game with me, make me feel better." He's saying I can't play on my own and I'm your responsibility, so make me happy. Mother, meanwhile, is ready to pull her hair out.

Depression has the same root as boredom. A husband asks his wife what's wrong and she says she's depressed or lonely. What she's really doing is calling for help, asking her mate to rescue her. The message the husband gets, however, is that she's blaming him for her problem, and that it's up to him to do something to make her feel better. She's saying, in effect, You married me and marriage was supposed to make me happy and it didn't and now I'm depressed and so you've failed. That's a powerful burden to lay on someone's shoulders. In placing that burden on others, the depressed person is drawing attention to herself and shifting responsibility elsewhere. Often, when someone says, "I'm depressed," the implied message is, "And it's not my fault."

So whose responsibility is it? In my experience, the problem is rooted in the human trait of expressing aggression. As I've said a hundred times, if a couple doesn't pay attention to their needs for aggression, they're going to begin attacking each other instead of their common enemies. We humans are pair-bonded creatures who tend to be monogamous. When the bond fails and monogamy loses its appeal, we do not hesitate to hate and attack whatever we view as worthless, especially our mates and ourselves.

Despite what most people believe, depression doesn't cause relationships to fail. On the contrary: *Problems in the relationship cause depression.* The depressed person considers herself lacking, unable to give to others; the truth is she's withholding herself, *unwilling* to give.

HUSBAND AND WIFE

We all have bad days, days when everything seems to go wrong—the car breaks down, we miss important appointments, dinner gets burned, etc. These days can be depressing, but they're an example of *situational depression,* a low mood caused by certain clear-cut events. When the circumstances are alleviated, so is the depression. Unfortunately, that's not the kind of depression that most people in destructive relationships suffer. For such people, depression is a constant, a way of life.

Mike comes homes and asks his wife Jill how her day went, and Jill says it's been terrible. "I'm depressed," Jill says. "I've been driving the kids around all day. I feel like a chauffeur. Then the car kept stalling and you know I've never been good at driving a car with a manual transmission and I felt like an idiot out there in traffic with those screaming brats." (Obviously in Jill's ideal personal world her cars don't stall.) "I don't understand how any man who earns the kind of money you do would let his wife drive a six-year-old car anyway. If you thought about me and the kids once in a while, you'd do more for us. It seems as if you don't pay any attention to me anymore." Poor Jill—the innocent victim of a counterfeit husband who obviously doesn't love her like she wants. And how convenient for her—she doesn't have to take responsibility for her emotions, she can project all her problems onto Mike. *He's* to blame, the S.O.B.

By the time a couple reaches this point in their marriage, there probably isn't too much anyone can do to save it. But if Mike had been paying close attention a few years ago, he might have seen some of the warning signs. He might have realized, for example, that Jill was trying to hold all her aggression inside her. She always seemed to get depressed over things that made most people merely angry. And if Jill finally *did* get angry, it was usually something extremely trivial. Once, for instance, their son forgot to turn off the light when he left a room and Jill launched into a tirade.

Everyone at times feels upset or unhappy. My daughter, for example, might have a bad day when her car breaks down, and she might be angry at herself for not knowing how to fix the car. This anger might even make her yell at the kids. But in another part of her mind she also sees what she's doing. She feels guilty for having screamed, guilty for being so hard on herself. Despite her temporary anger she catches herself acting irrationally. That ability to remain somewhat objective even during emotional turmoil is a healthy sign; it means that the anger or depression is not going to destroy her self-esteem.

For Jill, however, depression is a sign of intolerable failure. She feels helpless and empty, and projects her feelings of inferiority onto everyone around her. Instead of asking a neighbor to help her out by taking the kids to the movies, she tells them they can rot around the house for all she cares. She calls the friend she was supposed to meet for lunch, and cancels, and then mopes that she "never goes out and does anything fun." But then next day, even though the car is fixed, she doesn't bother to pick up the phone and make a date. That night she's too tired for sex, as she has been for months. Mike invites her to go with him to dinner next week for an executive retiring from his office, but she doesn't have energy to get her hair done or shop for a new dress. . . .

And so begins a long spiral into "depression." Depression leads to saying "no" to life. It's looking at a relationship that isn't all you expected it to be and devaluating your partner, "When I married you, I thought you were a loving, caring, nurturing man. What a terrible mistake I made. You made a fool of me." Depression is a mood state which is often simply the result of *not getting what we want* (or what we think we want.)

SAVING FACE

In a sense, depression is one of the most honorable medical diagnoses of modern times. In our society, there is even an element of intelligence and creativity associated with depression—the "moody" artist, the gifted but brooding and alcoholic writer, for example. Depression implies the person is still capable of functioning. God forbid I should write "suffers from anxiety" on your chart. Society would take that to mean you're a flake. And if I wrote "personality disorder"—well, you would really be branded. But depression—ah, that's safe and acceptable; you must be sensitive.

Since the 1960s, doctors have been diagnosing depression on a regular basis. Responding to this trend, drug companies began producing a slew of new medications they called antidepressants. There are so many antidepressants being developed it's hard to keep up with them.

Most of the people who come to me for help with problems in their relationships say that, at one time or another, their doctors told them they have a "chemical imbalance" and gave them a prescription for antidepressants. But depression is really a symptom, not the cause, of the problem. After a while, even if the drugs help, the person's basic personality impairments win out and they go right back to being depressed. To my way of thinking, taking antidepressants is ultimately just another way people have of avoiding self-knowledge and refusing to take responsibility for their happiness. Sure, drugs might relieve some of the symptoms, but the underlying problems are still untouched.

As we've seen, when we talk about "codependency," we're

talking about people whose basic personality structures are underdeveloped. When we say "depression," we're actually discussing the same thing. To understand depression, therefore, we have to trace its history in the formation of an individual's personality.

EARLY LOSSES

For the first year of life, the mother's breast represents and symbolizes all that is good in the infant's experience. That's why weaning is such a traumatic experience. But the actual mother is still there, offering reassurance, so gradually the child comes to terms with the good breast and the bad breast, the good mother and the bad mother. Ideally, she learns to accept that there's good and bad inside herself as well, and she unites these as she forms a stable self-image.

A year or two goes by. Susie, now a toddler, has to achieve separation once again. As we've seen, during this phase she'll cling to transitional objects, such as toys or teddy bears. As a slightly older toddler, Susie will turn to her father. As a child she forms close friends; as an adolescent she begins to date. Finally her mature bond with a person of her own generation permits her to relinquish her hold on the attachments of her childhood and provides a *lasting* substitute for the symbolic breast.

What I haven't pointed out in this scenario is that at each step Susie, like all of us, felt the temptation to regress. The temptation takes many forms: She might not have transitional objects (i.e. friends to play with) nor have a father to turn to. Deep down, she just wants to crawl back into Mommy's bosom. In adolescence she doesn't want to give up her love for Daddy and find someone all her own to love, since Daddy's loved her all these years and she knows she can at least trust his love. Whenever we are frustrated in our drive to become individuals, we want to give up, go back. We're looking for reassurance, for gratification, so that we may regress.

Children find ways around the developmental need to gain strength as an individual. One day at nursery school, for example, Tracy discovers another child playing with "her" toy. She looks around the room, unsure of herself, feeling extremely helpless. The teacher comes over and offers her a cookie. So Tracy holds back her tears and eats her cookie. Repeat this experience often enough, and Tracy will begin using food, or other addictive substances, as a defense against feeling helpless. Repeating the experience also means that Tracy is denied the chance of learning to use her own aggression in the relief of her helplessness.*

Except the experience isn't repeated. The next time Tracy finds another kid playing with the toy she wants, no one comes by to offer her a cookie. So Tracy starts to perform a dance in the middle of the floor, and the people around her stop to look, and they tell her how good she is. Or maybe she goes over to the teacher and tries to get her to throw the ball back and forth. If the teacher doesn't respond Tracy throws the ball herself and hits another girl on the back of the head with it. Once again, she's circumventing helplessness instead of dealing with it.

At home, it's a different story. Tracy's mother has her hands full with the younger children. Tracy senses the world no longer revolves around her. She could stand on her head but her mother wouldn't pay any attention. She feels like a failure. Tracy's never developed the capacity to separate the good mother from the bad mother, the good self from the bad self. For her, it's all or nothing. When she's angry, she turns her anger on the most readily available object—at school, it's the other children, but at home it's herself. She can't, after all, risk getting angry at her mother, can she? She can't afford to risk losing her, hence self abuse will be associated with the security of not losing mother.

There's a little of both Susie and Tracy in all of us. How well we manage to overcome frustrations, and accomplish the process of developing individual strengths, so that we can accept not getting what we want or having to give up unrealistic ideals, often protects against depression. For the person whose personality organization is poorly developed, such experiences lead to the feeling that one is alone; this leads to depression, which in turn usually leads to defenses against that depression. E.g., denial, splitting, idealizing, devaluing, projecting, physical pain, and controlling.

---

* Interestingly, here we see the seeds of an adult eating disorder, where the overeating will stuff anger, confirm helplessness, and deny one's need to recognize and employ their natural aggression.

MATURE SELF-ESTEEM

In Chapter Six, we saw how a person's ego attempts to root itself in reality while the superego (the conscience plus the "ego-ideal") strives for perfection. A person like Tracy, with her fragile personality, never really feels confident that she has lived up to her mother's expectations. But when Tracy grows up and finds a man to love her, that doesn't matter anymore. Having a significant other proves she's a very lovable person, no matter what she feels her mother thinks. She now feels a sense of omnipotence over her self doubts.

For awhile she feels appreciated and wonderful. But in another sense, things are *too* wonderful. Because her ego is underdeveloped, Tracy's sense of self-esteem depends entirely upon her partner's love for her. The husband she idealizes (and thus denies her ambivalent feelings toward) is thus able to take control of her own ego. She can't function alone, let alone cultivate a mature sense of herself. Tracy says that being in love is invigorating—she feels ecstatic, elevated, like she's floating on air. But in time all extremes turn to their opposites. What's the opposite of floating on air? Feeling "heavy" or "sinking" —both terms commonly used to describe depression.

All of a sudden Tracy becomes anxious that her husband might reject her. Maybe her fears have some basis, maybe not, but that isn't most important. What's important is her *fear*. Now, if she'd been in a mature relationship which included shared dependency and shared aggression, she could understand that all human relationships have to end, whether through abandonment or death, and could reconcile herself to that fact. That very knowledge would have deepened the love she and her husband felt for each other. But because of her exaggerated abandonment fears, Tracy never understands that. And now all she sees is that her ideal world is collapsing around her. For Tracy, as for many other people, the prospect of loss simply proves what she's known all along: she doesn't deserve to have good things, because she'll only spoil them.

By seeing herself as bad, Tracy is able to preserve her image of her "ideal" husband, hoping his virtues will carry her as they did in the past. But this also means giving up what little sense of her own goodness she has left. She gives up all hope of harmony between the ego (or real world) and the perfect world of the ego-ideal. Bliss is obviously unattainable. In doing so she becomes depressed. Sooner or later, she's going to tell herself: "I'd rather be dead." What she's really saying is "I wish *you* were dead, Mother." (Here, mother is seen as the source of all promises for pleasure). But her anger, expressed as a wish to kill her mother, is directed at herself. All suicidal thoughts begin as unconscious vengeance toward another person. Then her aggression, her anger, makes her feel guilty; guilt causes her to attack herself. As you might suspect, the affinity between depression and masochism is extremely strong.

PLEASING YOURSELF

We saw in Chapter Three how the toddler who has difficulty separating from mother usually shows less interest in the self-fulfillment possible through masturbation. The same holds true in adults: I've found that my patients who are suicidal and destructive in their relationships often report having difficulty masturbating as well. "I was thirty years old before I realized it was okay to touch myself," Tracy says. "And even now, I find it most pleasurable when I'm angry. It's like I'm attacking myself—so I can release something that's inside of me."

Frankly, it's no wonder that Tracy attacks herself. As we saw above, her identification with mother, her female identity is ambivalent at best, and she feels a deep-seated urge to "spoil" everything that is good. For Tracy, as for many other women with personality disorders, the vagina is bad. After all, it's in the same area as that dirty old anus. It's smelly. It's part of the "bottom," which gives off feces, urine, and blood. If she doesn't "spoil" she "soils." She remembers, as a child, how her mother gave her a laxative or enema every time she thought it necessary. Mommy owned her body, and could do whatever she wanted to it, including taking a hairbrush and swatting her with it until her bottom swelled. Tracy tried hard to control herself, not because she wanted to express her love for her mother but because she didn't want to be spanked or receive the enema. Her mother must be right: Her private parts were bad, dirty, and were nothing but a source of pain. Menstruation brought more pain; so did sex, even though she wouldn't let herself admit that. She once saw a film portraying the beauty of natural childbirth—it tried to show the vagina as soft, pink, moist, and sensual. Tracy found it disgusting.

RESUMING RESPONSIBILITY

If no one pays attention to someone's depression, that person is forced to assume responsibility for their actions. *And once they begin acting again, the depression goes away!* Whenever new patients join our therapy community, we ask them to say something about themselves, why they're here, and what the problem is that they want to work on. Virtually everyone says one of two things: either "I'm codependent" or "I'm depressed." We began to hear these terms so often they lost a great deal of their meaning. So we set a policy: You can't use either term. Instead you have to find different—and more accurate—ways to describe why you're in the hospital.

Under that policy, then, a lot of people begin by making revealing statements about their relationships. Jacqueline said, "I'm here because I can't find satisfaction in my marriage." Kim said, "I'm here because I've been unable to find happiness with one person. I keep hitting the singles bars and getting into short-term affairs, and now with AIDS and everything going around, I'm getting frightened." Other people come up with statements that show more insight into themselves. Pamela, for example, said: "I'm here because I'm unable to feel anything. I know I must be going through some pleasurable things and some awful things, but I'm not able to work up any emotion, no matter what. It's as if everything's all locked up inside me, and I don't know how to let it out." I find that the more people have to verbalize what they're going through, the more they're going to set it in a larger frame of reference and thus have a clearer picture of what's happening within them.

When Tracy came into the hospital, though, she was so clearly and severely depressed that I was tempted to let her use the word for a while. She struggled to express what was bothering her; finally she came up with "Depression's got a hold of me." I probed a little deeper: "What's got hold of you?"

"I don't know," she replied. "Depression—the chemicals in my brain are out of balance or whatever." We let it go at that. But for a few days we didn't let her use the word "depression" again. A week went by; then I asked Tracy what happened to the thing she was calling depression. She thinks for a long time and finally says "I give up."

"Is that why you're here, because you've given up?"

"Yeah, actually, you're right. I *have* given up."

Now *that* gave us something to work with. Tracy accepted responsibility instead of copping out by saying "Depression has taken over." With that as a clue, we began exploring the reasons she's given up.

JUST SAY NO

If you're paying attention to what's happening inside you, you can usually catch the "depression" before it takes root. Some people manage to tell themselves, "All of my feelings are important." "All of my feelings belong to me." "I need to know all of my feelings." And nine times out of ten, the thought of depression will go away. Why? *Because it didn't exist to begin with!* What you think is "depression" is nothing more than an excuse, a way of avoiding your aggressive nature, and the multiplicity of feelings associated with it, an attempt to force other people to do things for you. You don't acknowledge your aggression or energy to create a healthy sense of self-esteem, so you let your opinion of yourself depend totally upon what you *presume* other people are thinking about you.

I have always believed that if we could acknowledge our *wickedness,* we wouldn't have to deal with worthlessness. Depressed people *choose* to remain depressed. Feeling bad is safe for them, it's familiar. It's the smell of home. After all, many have been feeling depressed since childhood (although as youngsters they might have described the feeling as "boredom" or something like "helplessness"). By staying depressed, such people stay in control; they believe it's better to feel bad, and look good, than to *be* bad; they're able to continue denying their feelings of envy, greed, rage, and—most importantly—dependency. By seeing "depression" as only "bad," they assert their inability to tolerate ambivalence. They attempt to abolish differences, including the difference between the sexes. Their thoughts run something like this: "If I acknowledge that I'm attracted to—that I physically *need*—the opposite sex, then I won't be depressed, I'll be grateful. I can't handle 'grateful.' 'Depressed' is all I can manage." Here happiness is being alone, and depression is being with what's familiar.

SELF AND OTHER

In Chapter Six, we saw how destructive the marriage between Marge and Dennis had become. By that point Marge was more angry than depressed, but her need to project anger onto her husband stemmed from the same root as most depression: She wasn't able to have what she thought she wanted.

In order for a person to regain lost self-esteem, two things have to happen. First, the person must gratefully accept love (in the form of affection and tenderness) from another individual. Second, and perhaps more importantly, the person must work to achieve harmony between her realistic possibilities and her idealized self-image. So long as you'll only settle for looking good, or the Ideal Relationship, you don't stand a chance.

The mark of depressed people is that they don't stop, look, and listen in an effort to discover that all of their emotions are understandable and have a purpose. It's easier to keep lying to themselves and stay trapped in self-pity. The poor little girl who was deprived of oneness with her mother thinks she needs lots of sympathy now; but in truth she's making herself *more important* than mother ever was. Self-awareness is another matter; to be self-aware means we fully recognize the differences between what we are and what we would like to be. You can be free of depression when you base self-esteem on authentic feelings, not qualities you wish you had.

Having another person's affection will always make it easier for you to accept yourself. Being easier on yourself sometimes means you're not so quick to reject attention from another person; when you are more accepting, the other person becomes more willing to show affection. The conscious desire (as opposed to neediness) for the other's affection, accompanied by conscious gratitude for having it, are the foundations of self-esteem.

MOURNING

One way to show you how to regain your lost self-esteem is by comparing that process to the process of mourning. Our success in handling both depression and mourning spring from the internal images we have formed of our loved ones as well as ourselves.

As I've explained, when the toddler like Susie attempts to

strike out on her own, she has to come to terms with her internal images of her mother. Of course, the fact that she can always go back to her mother for reassurance helps immensely. But what happens if Susie's mother is away on business for two weeks? She may become much more reliant on her father's presence. She clings to a teacher she never paid much attention to before. What she's doing, in effect, is relying on other people to help her remember pieces of the "good mother." The adult grieving for a loved one goes through a similar process. The more friends and relatives she has around her to share her grief and to offer sympathy, the easier it will be for her to retain a memory of her loved one's goodness, and to restore harmony within her inner world.

In the process of mourning, we internalize the person who was lost. That means we work hard to build up the person's image inside us so that we don't miss their physical presence quite so much. The psychiatry books describe this process as *introjection*. In order to accomplish introjection, we draw upon our memories of the person we lost; we also replay all the fantasies of harm and reparation which have been with us since our earliest childhood. In mourning we are mending our despondency over an emptiness in the outside world. Whether the feelings are angry or sad, in mourning their object is external.

Depression is also associated with loss. There are more varied losses that can stir up feelings of helplessness, worthlessness, sadness, and grief. The hopelessness and worthlessness of the *self* distinguishes depression from grief. For example, we might suffer the loss of our exaggerated dreams, of our idealized picture of the world. Unless we develop the capacity to mourn, we will simply move from one idealized image to another, unable to face reality. In the process of mourning we rebuild our internal representations of other people as well as ourselves. In depression as in mourning, the more people around us who share our grief, who offer understanding and reassurance, the easier the process will be.

Lenore is a case in point. She meets Franklin at several church functions, and falls madly in love with him—from a distance, since Franklin is married. She hears that Franklin is in the process of getting a divorce. He's always pleasant and cordial, but never asks her out alone. Finally she can't stand it any longer, so she invites him to dinner. He leaves early. The next time she invites him, he refuses apologetically, saying he has other plans. She invites him to a party at her office; again, he has other plans. It's only after he refuses several invitations, that Lenore gives up any hopes of a budding romance. She becomes depressed over the loss for a short time, but she has a lot of other friends, and begins seeing them more often. Gradually she gets over both Franklin and her depression: the mourning process has been successfully accomplished.

Also, it is important to notice that Lenore was aggressive (move toward) in her half of this failed relationship. Both mourning and depression are far more difficult to resolve if we were passive in the experience of loss. Those who attempt suicide after a break up all know that they did not give it their best efforts. This guilt supplements the pain of the loss.

When idealizations of self and others are minimized and realities are accepted, we realize that we must always live at least in the shadow of despair. Traumas, losses, psychic pains, frustrations, and disruptions are inevitable. Total satisfactions are impossible. Confronted with our limitations we may either slide into depression or begin to use our aggression to take our sexual and dependency needs seriously. Since we *cannot* really expel our demons, why not make them precious to us (better I have them, than they have me).

Most psychotherapists would agree that to be orphaned, abandoned, or illegitimate are among the worst pains a child can experience. Stacking the odds against a productive life, one might say. To dramatize my point—that our demons (our aggressions) may become our friends—here is a sample list of such people who were abandoned: Tolstoi, Ghandi, Sartre, Kierkegaard, Plato, Aristotle, Dostoevski, Dante, Poe, Keats, Wordsworth, Michelangelo, and Dickens. Their despair led to creativity.

We have talked of how loss, of how not getting what we want, and of how devaluing idealized things, helps to create the mood state we call depression. Ideals aren't lost, they're given up, because we didn't realize that we could be understood—and equally important, that we could know ourselves much better.

9

The Past Reconsidered

Here's the voice of Frances G.:

"All my mother ever wanted was to have children. Once she had five kids she really no longer needed my father, so she just sort of closed herself off to him. As the oldest child, I used to look at their marriage and promise myself that would never happen to me. I was going to have a career, a family, and a great relationship with my husband.

"I already had my nursing degree before I married John, and I kept working up until the eighth month during each of my three pregnancies. I loved my kids, and gave them all the time and attention that I possibly could—short of quitting work. I tended to John, too. I made love with him any time he wanted, regardless of how tired I was. And I made sure he wanted me. I fed the kids early, then made dinner for the two of us, sometimes complete with candles.

"Then all of a sudden John comes in and announces he's found someone else and he wants a divorce. I felt like I'd been run over by a cement mixer. All my brothers and sisters are happily married. How come *I'm* the one who suffers?

"He's married again now, and he wants the kids to come live with them. He insists I don't love the kids because I won't quit my job. He's damn near got even *me* convinced. He can't grasp the fact that I'm head of the household now, and I couldn't quit even if I wanted to."

"I guess I was wrong to think I'd be able to do it all. I never learned anything about love, only how to smother people with affection and attention. Either that or I reject them completely. I thought as I grew up I could find some middle ground and unite the two, but I can't. I have no model, nothing to work from. If my mother were still alive, I'd wring her neck."

ONCE UPON A VICTIM

It happens every time: People who can't sustain a relationship view themselves as victims. They are victimized by abusive parents, or by parents who loved so much they couldn't let go. They were abandoned by a mother who died very young, or were sexually victimized by an uncle or teacher in childhood. A woman might claim she is the victim of a husband's drinking, an abusive husband, or a mother who's still interfering in her life. Or a man who served in Vietnam might say that he is the victim of the trauma he suffered there and thus he can't perform sexually.

My patients tell me that the word "victim" appears repeatedly in all the popular codependency literature. Even when it is not stated, it is certainly implied.

The term even haunts professional writing on the subject. In an article on role identity published in *The American Journal of Psychoanalysis*, F. Von Broembsen pinpoints four "roles" that adults who were victimized as children continually fall into:

The *caretaker* is someone who tries to replace a parent's inadequate mate. As adults, such people are always doing for others—and resenting it.

The *keeper of safe worlds* is someone who, both as a child and as an adult, will do anything to maintain harmony. In many cases these are the enablers who put up with, or even encourage, another person's addictions.

The *cat's paw* is a capable person who nevertheless is continually being exploited.

Lastly, the *spoiler* is a manipulative person who can't simply enjoy life but instead feels compelled to ruin happiness for others as well.

Actually, seeing oneself as a victim is little more than just another way of shirking responsibility. It's odd, too: victims seem to parrot the same types of remarks that depressed persons say: "it's not my fault!" "It seems so hopeless, I can't help myself!" "Do something for me!" Once a victim, always a victim. There's one thing missing from Frances G.'s assessment of her past: If her mother was such a source of suffering, how is it that her siblings have overcome the past and managed to maintain happy marriages?"

DIFFERENT CHILDHOODS

When they were kids, Frances's two sisters often brought friends home to play or listen to records or just gossip and giggle. Not Frances—she was too ashamed. She didn't want her friends to see how her mother watched over her and criticized her every move. Or she was afraid her father might come home early and her friends would see how awfully her mother treated him. Her sibs might go running off to the movies or to the playground. Not good old Frances—she might not like it very much, but she knew her mother would be beside herself with anger and sadness if none of the kids was home to keep her company. So Frances did the dutiful thing. She stayed.

In hearing Frances recount her sad tale, I noticed a thread that seemed to tie a lot of things together. What Frances needed most as a child was reassurance—from other relatives, from the mothers of her schoolmates, from teachers. She seemed to enjoy attracting attention to herself: "Look how much I'm doing, look how wonderful I am, am I prettier than my sisters?" She couldn't go and play with friends; she had to stay home and keep Momma company to be there when Daddy came home. But what a convenient excuse for not having to assert herself, for not going out and *making* friends. And really, when I thought about it, she was extremely lucky to have the mother she did; because when you came right down to it, Frances simply didn't trust herself to function on her own.

And that, in a nutshell, is how Frances differed from her siblings. Her brothers and sisters had problems, to be sure, but they still wound up with fully formed personalities. They enjoyed being with other people, but they didn't depend on having someone else to lean on. Reconciled to their own ambivalent feelings, they didn't need someone else onto whom they could project all their "badness." They didn't have to find someone to blame in order to value themselves.

Frances did. In considering her case, I often wonder: Who

was the truer "victim" of this unhealthy relationship—Frances? Or the mother whom she was so compelled to compete with.

OTHER VICTIMS

Let me tell you about George, a patient who blames all his problems on his experience in Vietnam. He saw children carrying bombs, he saw women prostituting themselves to get a bowl of rice or a pack of cigarettes, he saw death and destruction ... and it was all too much for him. But a lot of men went to Vietnam, and most of them returned still fully capable of functioning in society. The question is not what happened to them in Vietnam—*it's what they took with them when they went there*. The ones who came back claiming their self-assurance had been destroyed probably had little or no self-assurance in the first place. George beat his wife, frequently, *both* before and after Vietnam.

As far as I'm concerned, people who play the "victim" give themselves permission to ignore the ways that their own internal shortcomings contribute to their problem. I'm not alone in this view. Dr. Janine Chasseguet-Smirgel, for example, has observed that all masochists, paranoids, psychotics, and narcissists believe themselves to be innately good and that bad comes from external sources. Projecting your hostility onto another person confirms your own goodness before it points to another person as the source of trouble. Victims, therefore, manage to convince themselves that they are not bad, even when they cause harm to their persecutors.

Until you are willing to confront your internal conflicts, you're going to continue being "victimized." You may find that the seeds of destruction in your failed relationships were planted by your own hand.

ADULT VICTIMS AND SAVIORS

Shirley, sexually abused in childhood, vowed that she would never again be so powerless. She always picks lovers who need her desperately—because they can't stop drinking, or taking drugs, or whatever. Then she sets about "rescuing" them, and for a while she feels good about herself. Until finally the tables turn—her lover screams to just leave him alone, he doesn't want her help. And Shirley feels taken advantage of once again. She's so angry she could kill. No longer a rescuer, she becomes an "avenging harpy."

Noreen, with her immature personality, doesn't want to risk having her lover leave her. So she suppresses her own feelings and works hard to be precisely what she thinks he wants her to be. Then, to her surprise (but not mine), her lover browbeats her, mocks her, laughs at her. It's obvious she finds it better to be humiliated than rejected.

Both of these women are extremely manipulative in their own ways. They're involved in a kind of master-slave relationship. And for many such people, master and slave are continually changing places. At some points, they have to be in control and they have to abuse another person in the same way they were abused. But at other times, when they're not suffering, they feel lost and empty; as a result they force other people to abuse them. What it all comes down to is that *they knew how bad this relationship was going to be before they entered into it.*

Why did they marry a drug addict or an abusive person to begin with? There are lots of possible answers: Because they needed an outlet for their own destructive urges. Because as children they failed to develop the capacity to love. Because they never learned how to acknowledge their dependent and aggressive natures. They rebelled in adolescence but still couldn't stand on their own. Now they're married and still victimized. So they go to Alanon meetings. They get advice from friends. They meditate. They read book after book on codependency. Finally they detach. They divorce. They walk out. They think they want to be independent, but before too long they're right back where they started with someone who needs "saving." And no matter how bad it is, it's better than being ignored, alone, or just plain numb.

SELF-FULFILLING FANTASIES

Before people can feel comfortable with their sexual identity, they have to take ownership of their bodies. Without that sense of acceptance, sexuality becomes nothing more than an instrument for repairing a faulty sense of self-esteem. The act of masturbation may confirm feelings of separateness and autonomy, and the fantasy we experience during the act expresses how we feel about that separateness. The fantasies of most people who suffer from relationship failure reveal unresolved issues of dependency or aggression, but they seldom express mutual, shared contentment.

Shirley admits she masturbates a lot, and her fantasy clearly reveals her controlling tendencies. In the fantasy she created during the time she was involved in her last relationship, Shirley imagines herself lying naked on the bed, touching herself, while a large, handsome man sits on the chair, looking over his newspaper and smiling, pretending he isn't paying attention to her. Now that she is not in a relationship, her most frequent fantasy is of a faceless man who has an enormous penis. They've just finished making love, with him entering her from behind, and now he's coming toward her, facing her. The two of them are screaming obscenities at each other.

Noreen doesn't masturbate very often, "mainly because I'm afraid my husband will find out about it," she says. "But when I do, the other person begins by stimulating my breasts. Then the hands, just the hands, move lower. I can't see the person very clearly. In fact, I really can't tell if it's a man or a woman. I'm just lying there, extremely passive. I feel almost afraid to breathe, for fear I'll ruin it."

REGRESSION THERAPY

My patients tell me that practically all the literature on codependency talks about finding the "inner child" within you. One patient said, "When a book tells me how to find the 'inner child,' it sounds like they want me to perform an elementary kind of do-it-yourself hypnosis." You're supposed to peer inside your soul until you find the innocent child who felt so unloved. Then you cuddle that child, you tell her how much you love her. The inner child is, after all, always good; she is innocent and pure. In a perceptive article in *The New York Times Book Review*, Wendy Kaminer observes that this "inner child" appears to be just like "the most sentimentalized Dickens characters." Apparently, when you tell this inner child you love her, you're saying what your parents needed to say to you and never could.

Simple, isn't it? It's almost like cuddling and talking to a teddy bear to make yourself feel secure once again—even though mother has deserted you.

The truth is, it's not so simple.

Let's go back and take a closer look at that teddy bear. You didn't really love that bear, you simply controlled it. You did everything with it you wanted to do with your mother: you slept with it *whenever you wanted to*; you held it *whenever you wanted to*; you talked to it *whenever you wanted to*. You also abandoned it when you found a cuddlier one or a bigger one. Most teddy bears suffer severe damage: their stuffing is half gone, "someone" has pulled their eyes off. And that bear that was so important throughout childhood, where is it now? I searched all through my parents' house a few years ago, but I couldn't find mine. I haven't the slightest idea what became of it.

If it's anything like this teddy bear, the "inner child" isn't going to be comforted. When you find it, you're only going to subject it to more abuse. Loving the inner child might make you feel better for a short time. But in the long run you're doing yourself no favors, because you're still attempting to deny your aggressive nature, you're still trying to idealize a relationship—*and an imaginary one at that*. Who's kidding whom?

INTERNAL MOTHERS

It's a basic fact: Problems experienced in adult relationships always mirror and reflect the problems between the parent and the child. But, as that ragged, eyeless Teddy bear proves, *it's not the internal child who needs to be loved—it's the internal mother, and you still have a lot of hostility toward her*.

If you want to free yourself of codependency, you've got to recognize your mother's voice inside you. She still makes you feel guilty all the time. You feel guilty because you're trying so hard to please her, you need her love so badly, and nothing you do seems good enough. And guilt, of course, controls aggression; so long as you feel guilty, you're not going to assert yourself.

You're too old now to torture a helpless teddy bear, but you've found a human outlet for all your anger. Destructive relationships *originate* from the conflict with the internal mother, but they are consciously *experienced* through contact with the people around us. Melanie Klein points out that when we identify with our adult partners, and make certain sacrifices on their behalf, we are actually playing the part of the "good parent." We do everything for our partner we wished our parents had done for us. We are also able to play the part of the good child, the perfect child our parents would never let us be, appreciating all the sacrifices our partner is making for us.

A healthy relationship with our partners consists of both reality and fantasy. Internally, the fantastic images we formulate of the good and bad partner resemble those conscious and unconscious fantasies of the good and bad mother. When we sense that the figures in our inner world are being protective and loving toward us, we are able to project our own love toward a partner. But if the inner mother is perceived as harsh, demanding, and unloving, then we find it difficult to be at peace with ourselves. As a result we're continually frustrated in our adult relationships.

There's one crucial difference between the present and the past: as adults, we have the mental and emotional resources we need to reformulate these internal parental images and transform them into something positive and healthy. The trick is to first acknowledge our shared needs for dependency and aggression. If we can do that, we will have access to the happiness we seek in our relationships.

10

Shedding Light on Yourself

Imagine yourself in the middle of a long black alley. You can see light at either end. You hear noises around you. Should you run to the right? To the left? Should you flatten yourself against a wall and try not to breathe? The best thing that could happen would be if somebody turned on the lights. Then you could at least get a clear sense of what you're dealing with.

If you're like other people, by the time you admit your relationship isn't working, you're pretty frightened and confused. You may talk to friends, maybe even go to an Alanon meeting. But each person you talk to seems to give you a different—and conflicting—opinion. You don't know where to turn. You're so rattled trying to decide what you should do that you end up not doing anything at all. You wish someone would turn on the lights so you could see clearly!

Well, I want to help by shedding light on *"yourself."*

You're seeking help because the person you've married, or are living with, hasn't turned out to be all the things you expected. But frankly, I'm not interested in how he abuses you, how he has all these affairs outside the marriage, how much he drinks or how many drugs he takes. I'm interested in *you*. I want to find out what there is in your personality which made you choose a person who couldn't return your "love."

That's what psychotherapists are attempting to do with codependent patients: shed more light on the darkness that's frightening you. You enter treatment because you want more insight into *your* situation. You want to develop a better understanding of what's going on in *your* internal world.

MIXED BLESSINGS

When you make the decision to get help, it may seem at first that you have lots of options open to you. For example, go to your bookstore and you'll see scads of self-help books on the subject. Obviously I believe such books can be of value, or I wouldn't be writing this one. My patients who read those books tell me, however, that they try to do what the books say but still get nowhere with their relationships.

In her article for *The New York Times Book Review*, Wendy Kaminer astutely observes that such books "[exploit] readers' fears of embarking on the search for self without the aid of exercises, techniques, assurances of success and, of course, support groups. This isn't individualism so much as the hunger to belong."

That hunger to belong has led to the rise of self-help groups in recent years. Such groups are designed to offer encouragement and nurturance—extremely important for a person who finds herself receiving little or nothing from her partner. On a day-to-day basis, self-help groups can help you cope better with what's happening in your relationships. Support groups help you deal with the symptoms without touching the sickness that's causing them.

Consider what happened to Maureen. She's been married for ten years and her husband shows almost no interest in her. All he cares about is going out drinking and running off to hotels with prostitutes. She goes to her first Alanon meeting, and is justifiably upset. Everyone advises her to take care of herself, to "detach." A few people suggest she find more interests outside the home. They tell her alcoholism is a disease, and there's nothing she can do about that. What if she found herself married to a diabetic, would she try to change him? Of course not. The only thing she can do anything about is herself.

Maureen goes along with this for a while, but she soon realizes it's not really the answer. Detachment has its uses; if nothing else, it gives her some breathing room so she can take stock of herself. But what's the next step? Maureen doesn't want to just detach—she either wants to be happy with her husband or she wants the marriage to end. She was hoping to find someone who'd help her understand whether or not there was anything in the marriage worth saving. And if she ends this marriage, she doesn't want to repeat her mistake by entering into yet another codependent relationship. Though she finds it hard to pinpoint exactly, she has an innate sense that what's going on in her life might not be entirely her husband's fault.

At their most insightful, even the greatest proponents of self-help groups realize there's still a lot of work to be done. Melodie Beattie who first brought the problem of codependency to many people's awareness, is beginning to rethink her earlier statement that "Recovery is not only fun, it is simple." Self-help program for codependents have been around long enough now that people are becoming increasingly aware that recovery isn't exactly fun and is hardly simple.

PSYCHIATRIC DIFFERENCES

For far too long, during the sixties and seventies, psychiatrists and psychotherapists relied on therapeutic shortcuts such as tranquilizers, antidepressants, biofeedback, relaxation, self-hypnosis, or "daily affirmations." Therapists promised cures in the form of short-term supportive psychotherapy, sexual-abuse groups, woman's groups, primal scream therapy (emotional catharsis), sex therapy, and crisis clinics. The depth of the human personality and its relevance to relationship failure was for the most part ignored. But the best therapists are now correcting that situation.

The patients we're seeing today have different types of problems than the ones we saw twenty-five years ago, when I first began my practice. Today, most patients—male and female—have personality disorders of differentiating type and severity. Their ways of relating sexually are different from those of the neurotic patient. People with under-developed personalities, such as I've described in this book, have pregenital conflicts. Their problems stem mostly from the way they deny their aggressive side. Consequently they're much more prone to find perverse sexual solutions to deny their inability to fall in love and remain in love.

The majority of people who go through failed relationships are unable to love and are overwhelmed with unacknowledged hate. Perverted sexuality—idealizing love, adultery, sexual toys, degrading acts and fantasies, eroticized hatred—offers an easy, temporary solution. Instead of desiring union with each other, these people act alone, seeking pleasure by the shortest route. The quest for pleasures and ideals is matched by the need to deny that the darkness of life, is in fact a side of themselves.

THE SECRET IS OUT

My experience dealing with hundreds of patients over the years has convinced me of a basic fact, at once simple and complex:

Most codependents actually suffer from a recognized psychiatric condition known as borderline personality disorder.

Now, there was a time when psychotherapists were cautioned to keep such insights to themselves, but that's all changed in recent years. Today we know that patient education is one of the best forms of treatment we can offer.

Let me tell you more about borderline personality disorder (or BPD, for short.) I do so not to scare you but to inform you. As you no doubt realize, the first step in getting better is to give a name to the problem. Once you know what your enemy is, you can better figure out how to defeat it.

In his book *A Consumer's Guide to Psychiatric Diagnosis*, Dr. Mark A. Gould defines borderline personality disorder as "a disturbance in thinking and behaving that disrupts relationships with other people and that leads to intense, misdirected anger, mood swings, feelings of emptiness, inability to tolerate being alone, and actions that cause harm to oneself or others." That puts it in a nutshell.

BPD is the most common form of personality disorder, affecting up to one out of every four psychotherapy patients. It strikes women at least three times as often as men—the ratio is even greater in my codependency therapy groups.

Studies of the families of people with BPD have shown conclusively that the parents tend to be either absent or neglectful, failing to provide adequate support, attention, and discipline, or they are overinvolved, as demonstrated in the way they resist or punish their children's efforts to become independent.

In some cases, the symptoms of BPD let up as the person reaches their forties. Often, however, the symptoms persist. When they do, the person continues to seek to fill a sense of inner emptiness by forming relationships that contain strong sadomasochistic tendencies.

People with BPD fit most of the following descriptions:

- Intense, unstable relationships that swing between idolizing and loathing the other person
- Impulsiveness that shows up in self-destructive ways such as overspending, careless sexual behavior, drug and alcohol abuse, shoplifting, fast driving, or binge eating
- Sudden, short-lived mood swings marked by irritability, depression, fear, and nightmares
- Frequent temper outbursts, relentless anger, or crying spells
- Self-harming thoughts and behavior such as suicide attempts or self-mutilation
- Uncertainty about one's own identity manifested in such ways as concern about self-image, sexual preference, career choice, long-term goals, values, or friends
- Persistent feelings of emptiness or boredom
- Frenzied efforts to avoid abandonment, whether the threat of abandonment is real or not.

People with borderline personalities are very idealistic—on the surface. Underlying those ideals, however, is a lot of destructive behavior. They see everything as either "good" or "bad." They're not willing to tolerate any ambivalence. People with BPD either love or hate the people they're involved with. But, because they're not willing to admit their own capacity for hatred, they project it onto the people around them. Everything's is "someone else's fault," never their own. But as I've shown throughout this book, idealizations are extremely dangerous.

If you are suffering from codependent relationships, the most important insight you could have into yourself is to find out how you idealize things—*and why*.

If you're thinking of getting therapeutic help, I strongly advise you to look for a therapist who understands the concept of personality formation and is committed to helping *you* understand it. Any good therapist is going to shed light on your idealizing and projection tendencies, point out where the dangers are, and respect you at the same time to make you less afraid to look. There is absolutely nothing wrong with being supportive, but it's important that support doesn't become one more means of denying reality.

ONE TREATMENT MODEL

Once you make the commitment to enter therapy, any good therapist who meets the above qualifications should be able to work well with you on an outpatient basis. But I like to think of an inpatient program such as we've developed at NorthShore Psychiatric Hospital as a sort of "boot camp"—it provides that initial insight and gets patients off to a head start, and speeds up the long recovery process. While this is at present the only program of its kind that I know of, hopefully other hospitals will be developing similar programs in the not-too-distant future. In the meantime, telling you about how treatment takes place at our facility will give you an understanding of what you can expect—or even demand—from your own treatment program.

As I've said continually: when you fall in love, you're supposed to feel happy. A healthy relationship gives you a good feeling you've never had before.

By contrast, most of the people who enter our program claim that, in their experience, love is "the same *old* feeling." Instead of expanding, they're just recreating an old experience in a new relationship. Psychologically speaking, their spouses represent the internalized images of their parents; codependents form relationships in an effort to tie up developmental loose ends. Our job is to study why those ends are still loose, and to discover how they can be tied up in healthier ways.

I feel strongly that, for most people, the experience of caring for someone else and being cared for by that person is the ultimate definition of happiness. The theme of our program, then, is to assess patients' mental health on the basis of their ability to feel good in a relationship.

WORKING UP INTEREST

If our program has one goal, it's getting people to become acutely interested in themselves. Maureen, for example, comes into our program, and the first day she tells me about her childhood, what her life was like before she met her husband. I'll ask something like, "What was it like when you first realized there was a difference between boys and girls?" Maureen starts to tell me about how her mother explained the difference. I stop her. "No, I'm not interested in what your *mother* said, I want to know *how you* experienced it." And the majority of people are taken aback—no one's ever asked them these things about themselves before, no one's ever cared how they experienced things (including themselves).

As I listen, I begin to detect the unconscious patterns that run throughout Maureen's life. I'm not only interested, I'm fascinated by her past, and I'm going to share my fascination with her. I care about her, and I respect her, but I can't magically change things. All I can do is stimulate her interest in her private inner self.

One day during the second week of her stay Maureen comes up to me and asked how long it would be before her depression lifted. Well, I couldn't answer that. I explain that depression sets in when we're trying to deny stronger emotions. Maureen was making her depression the scapegoat, divorcing it from its companion emotions, making an idol out of something that was supposed to save her. Sure, it would be painful to face it, but there's little growth without pain. If she could reunite depression with its companion emotions, the whole picture would become clearer.

All of a sudden, Maureen becomes fascinated, too. Four weeks later, when she leaves the program here and continues therapy as an outpatient, she not only has more insights into herself, but she finds her unconscious fascinating. She's anxious to know more about it, and thus more about herself. And she's not afraid any longer. There's too many interesting things going on inside her; she has no interest in devoting such energy to her fears.

"You know something, Doctor?" Maureen said one day. "When I first went to Alanon meetings, people were telling me I had to learn to love myself, and I swear that comment made my hair stand up. Well, I was talking to a friend from Alanon this morning, and she made that comment. This time I really understood what she meant. I have a feeling I even understand it better than she does."

PSYCHIATRIST AND PATIENT

I interview each patient when they first enter the program. I also schedule a therapy session with them once or twice a week during their five- or six-week stay. Usually an hour and a half each. All patients are also assigned to a primary therapist (usually a psychologist or social worker) who meets with them for one hour sessions three times a week during their hospitalization, and continues to see them on as outpatients after they leave. In addition to these private sessions, the "therapeutic community"—all the patients plus all the staff—meets for an hour every day. There are many groups and classes throughout the waking hours of each week.

The first session, I take what we call a developmental history. I'm interested in knowing about the parents: Were they around much when you were growing up? What people actually cared for you in the first years? Was abandonment experienced? Were brothers or sisters born at times when your intimacy with Mother was crucial? As I've been alluding to throughout this book, people's ability to stand alone, to accept their dependent and aggressive natures, depends upon their ability to separate from the mother. The answers to these questions give me a quick overview of how that process might have been interrupted. When Maureen, for example, tells me her mother was divorced and remarried three times before Maureen started kindergarten, I realize that the relations between mother and daughter must not have been very consistent. It would have been difficult for Maureen to come to a point where she could comfortably internalize both the good and the bad aspects of mother.

As she develops, the first difference the child has to appreciate is the difference between the mother and herself. Second is the sexual difference between boys and girls. If the first goal hasn't been accomplished—if a girl still wants to be fused with the mother—she's going to have problems when she notices the difference between her body and her brother's. And, of course, you have to fully accept and admire the differences between the sexes before you can establish a successful monogamous relationship. When the differences between the sexes, or between the generations, is denied, perversion is born. The desire to possess or be possessed takes the place of that all-important sharing.

Then I move on to explore the patient's transition into puberty. And what I'm interested in is when the body began to change from that of a child to that of an adult. More importantly, how did the patient perceive that change? If a boy has a good identification with his father, he's going to welcome the events, as will a girl who had good identification with mother. I'll ask my patients about their first dates, the first menses, what it was like when they lost their virginity (? physical union or bodily intrusion?). Of course, what I'm trying to do is trace the relationship patterns in the person's life, trying to uncover the landmark events that will most likely reveal conflict and frustration.

We then study the history of the patient's relationships up until the present moment. We focus mainly on successes and failures in relationships, and also what's going on sexually. The adult sexual thoughts, fantasies, and behaviors reveal a lot about how patients were affected by their first experiences of love and dependency upon the parents. As I've explained, they also reveal how well the patients achieved separation from that first bond. Often, I can detect in the pattern of sexual behavior signs of deep-seated but hidden hostility.

By the end of the first interview I've formulated a pretty clear impression of what the patient idealizes, what she's angry about, and how these factors affect her relationships. This is the material the patient and I will be working with for the rest of her stay in the hospital and during all of our future therapy sessions.

As an objective person and a trained therapist, I'm able to see the connections and patterns behind these events. Surprisingly, the patterns I see may be diametrically different from what the patient sees. In treatment, we refer to this as "the experience of opposites." For example, a woman might claim that she desperately wanted her father's love, whereas her stories reveal that the father was the more stable one and it was her *mother's* love she was always unsure of. Part of my goal, then, is to help her realize and understand this conflicting reality.

THE PRIMARY THERAPISTS

In the early stages of treatment I deal primarily with the patient's developmental past. At the same time the patient's primary therapists are often dealing with the patient's present. They devote many sessions to exploring the destructive tendencies in the patient's current relationship.

I make it clear to my patients that "My interest is in only you, and I want to focus only on you." Because I believe the patient needs one person to take this approach. The primary therapists, on the other hand, involve the patient's partner right away (assuming the patient is currently in a relationship). Every Tuesday night is family night, and the primary therapists usually see a patient along with his or her significant other at least once a week.

My background is in psychoanalysis, whereas most of our staff therapists were trained in behavioral and cognitive therapy. The element that connects these disciplines is the central theme of codependency: the human need for aggression. Having psychoanalysts working on the same team as behaviorists brings together the seminal thinking of those scientific pioneers, Freud and Darwin.

Community sessions run for an hour every morning, after which the staff meets alone for ten minutes. During those staff periods, we don't talk about the patients, we talk about ourselves. There are about fifteen psychologists and social workers on our team, many of them women. The main thing I look for in recruiting women, apart from solid academic skills and an ability to work with patients, is that they feel comfortable with their own aggression. All these women are very aggressive, but also extremely comfortable with their femininity. It's a healthy blend some patients never realized was possible until they encountered the role models offered by the primary therapists.

LOOKING TOGETHER

Another requirement for a potential member of our therapeutic team is that he or she is comfortable confronting patients.

The Latin roots of the word "confront" mean "facing together." In therapy sessions, we take a good look at our patients, then put what we see in front of them so that they can see it too. The act of doing so can be pretty scary. That's why we make sure our confrontations are motivated by love and concern for the person. I tell the staff, "If you are angry about something that's going on in your own life, *you dare not confront a patient*. If you don't like a certain patient, *don't confront her*. I tell them that I have to trust my own feelings before I can confront. There's no therapeutic value—in fact there may be therapeutic harm—in a confrontation staged between two people who have no common ground on which to stand.

I spent some time confronting Maureen about the reasons

she's stayed with her abusive husband for ten years. I remarked that she must need somebody to hate, so she's picked somebody with whom she obviously doesn't have to deal with the issues that loving and being loved bring up. At the end of the session I said: "Now I don't want you going out of the room thinking Dr. Thornton's saying you've got to hate. That's not the solution. But what I'm saying is, it's essential that you understand the hate is in there and what it's about, so you stop attacking yourself with your self-destructive thoughts and your suicide attempts. The reason the hate is so powerful in you is that it has not been properly acknowledged and balanced with love. And you do need a lot of loving." Such remarks are confrontational and supportive at the same time. That's what I'm constantly aiming for, even though the "support" side might not always be as apparent to the patients, at first.

PLACES AT THE TABLE

The program at our hospital has a unique feature we call "the table." During community sessions we all sit around this imagined table, much as a family would at dinner. This setting produces many surprising and often dramatic moments.

I always sit in the same place, at the head of the table. A psychologist, Dr. Stubblefield, sits across from me. The other staff members and patients array themselves around the table. Quite naturally, such positioning has determined the tone of some of the interactions that take place: We become in many ways a family. I am quite literally a father figure sitting at the head of table; Dr. Stubblefield, a woman, becomes the mother at the opposite head. The other staff members often fall into the roles of brothers and sisters, aunts and uncles. Through our interactions we represent a family experience for each patient. In essence, there's a lot of projection going on. And through these projections, patients gain access to their internalized parent figures.

"I want to disagree with what you just said, but I'm afraid to," Maureen comments to Dr. Stubblefield. "I'm afraid of Dr. Stubblefield's voice, the way she says things as if she's so sure of herself."

"Maureen, might there have been a person in your childhood or adolescence whom the doctor reminds you of?"

Suddenly a light clicks on. Maureen remembers her mother

after she married for the fourth time. "This guy was the one my mother was 'absolutely certain sure' would work out," she tells us. "She was so positive of herself, her voice developed a confidence I'd never heard before. I was seven or eight at the time. Mom was terrified that I was going to do something that would ruin all her happiness, so she became stricter with me than she'd ever been before." Needless to say, the marriage didn't last. Maureen picked up the signal from her mother: She hadn't been well-behaved enough.

Sometimes a patient will remark that she is afraid of me. When we explore this fear, we may find that I remind the patient of her father sitting at the head of the dinner table forcing her to eat, or threatening if she didn't do exactly as he wanted.

Lately, I've noticed that we spend a lot of time in community sessions talking about fathers. With the 50 percent divorce rate in this country, with children of both sexes growing up in the absence of fathers or father-figures, abnormal sexuality seems to be increasing as well. As we saw in previous chapters, if the father was perceived as weak, the woman will be unlikely to recognize the dangers to her developing self. Often she grows up unable to love a man but unable to say no to any man who asks. It's also very unlikely that she'll enjoy masturbation.

Women whose fathers were completely absent will often work hard to *deny the possibility* of danger. They attempt to destroy anything that represents what the father stands for, including reason, law, and patience. Having never learned to wait, they take impulsive shortcuts to utopia. These are the women who most often marry a physically abusive man, a drug addict, or a man who's extremely controlling.

For the male patient with a weak or absent father, waiting is even less of an issue. After all, he never had to wait for full possession of his mother's body, even with his infant genitals. More than likely, he never feared castration, because he never acknowledged the differences between the sexes or the generations. It was never necessary for him to integrate sexuality with tenderness.

PROJECTING

As we saw at the end of Chapter 5, in a healthy relationship partners can often become respected parents and grateful children for each other, achieving the fulfillment and understanding they never could with their real parents. With this partner it's okay to be dependent, okay to express our anger. But the majority of people who enter our program have never felt this security in a relationship. The therapeutic environment is the first place they achieve this insight, because they feel safe in the program.

These insights, and the patients' excitement about them are what we hope to achieve during residency. If outpatient therapy continues to be rewarding, after a year or more a startling transformation will take place. The therapist becomes a representation of the internal object—that is, the mother or the father, whichever is needed to complete the separation process. In psychotherapy terms, this is known as "transference." The patient's external object remains the husband or wife, the person they're involved with or hope to become involved with.

Here, again, is where psychotherapy takes things a step further than the popular literature on codependency can. No, we say, it's not important that you come to terms with your living mother. In my case, for example, my mother is seventy-plus years old and nearly blind. That's not the "mother" who's inside me. My internal mother, the mother I needed to achieve separation from as I grew, is a twenty-three-year-old girl, as she was when I was three years old.

The therapeutic process permits you to take another look at this internal mother. The more you come to terms with the past, the less you resent her. After all, she's exactly like you are, as was her mother before her. She's dependent, she's angry, but that's part of the human condition, and you can empathize with that because you're now admitting your own dependence and aggression. As a person matures, the need for a *gratifying* parent changes to the need for a *strong* parent. This explains why, as adults, frustration, deprivation, and aggression are often tolerated better than weakness. After all, if mother holds her own in an argument with you, you at least recognize after the fight is over that she's still healthy, still alive. You didn't damage her with your own expression of aggression. You might still feel contempt, but what you need is something more on the order of commiseration. With the internal mother there to reassure and console you, you finally develop the capacity to mourn the past and get on with your life in the present.

ACKNOWLEDGING SEPARATION

We had oneness when we were in the womb. We had oneness in early life. As adults it's essential that we acknowledge our separate existences. But for people suffering from borderline personality disorders, that process was halted at some point before they were able to separate. As adults, the struggle to separate continues to show itself in destructive relationships.

People come to see me who are already on their second and third marriages. They realize they have to approach this marriage (or the next one) differently, but don't know what to do. They don't want to be hurt again, or to continue hurting their children. Before a patient leaves the residential program, they realize how far they've come in that separation process—and learn how far they still have to go.

Typically, people with BPD feel dominated by mood swings. They might feel great when they leave the hospital, but over the next week, or month, or year, or decade, they're going to have ups and downs. Here, the mood *has them*, rather than they have a mood. The difference that therapy makes, however, is that they can *accept and understand* their varying moods. They have learned to accept themselves with the fringe benefits of simultaneously learning to accept other people's moods for what they are. The recovering codependent doesn't have to brand other people as "bad" just because they're physically or emotionally unavailable at the moment. Once patients discover how to acknowledge the difference between what they "need" and what they "feel," they begin trusting their ability to make reparation.

As a codependent seeking to get better, treatment offers you many valuable things. Through well-founded, well-guided therapy, you will learn how to shift your arrested development back into gear. The result will be increased maturity—not just for you but for the other half of your codependent relationship as well. Therapy shows you how to free your individual creativity so you can apply new solutions to old problems. Learning how to separate moves helps you graduate to the genital phase of development. Love becomes something you can both give and receive. True union with a partner at last becomes possible. You're no longer demanding or controlling; you're no longer afraid of forfeiting your identity.

When you abandon your historical reasons for remaining in a sick relationship, one of two things may happen: You may experience intolerable stress, or you may discover intense togetherness. As Dr. Kernberg has pointed out, successful resolution of codependency will either "dissolve the marriage or permit its re-creation on a new basis."

In either case, you win: You will either have the strength to cut your losses and move on to a new phase in your life, or you will recreate your relationship without codependency and thus without needless pain.

11

Society Reconsidered

As I browsed in the card store last week, a card in the Juvenile Birthday rack caught my eye: "Son," it said, "you make weekends special!"

Obviously the intended recipient of such a card is a child whose parents are divorced and who sees one of them, probably his father, only on weekends. "Son," whoever he turns out to be, is one of the luckier children; at least his father lives close enough to spend time with him, even if it is only two days out of the week.

The availability of such a card is just one reflection of the shake-up our society is experiencing as a result of a divorce rate around 50 percent. When a social trend has reached the point where a greeting card company gets in on the act, you know it's pretty deeply entrenched. Many couples are so sure that their marriage will end that they sign prenuptial agreements to handle the situation when it finally occurs. I can see it now, the latest card from Hallmark: "Congratulations on signing your prenuptial agreement." We are rapidly facing the consequence of raising children without parental stability nor security. Whether it be absent mothers, absent fathers or multiple mothers, multiple fathers. The likelihood is highly probable that the child will grow up to repeat the same unstable patterns in his efforts to gain mastery of his painful insecurity and of his fear of abandonment.

Divorce where children abruptly lose a parent is just one of many trends buffeting our society. Another trend is the change in the quality and quantity of mothering due to the increase of working women and the impact that it has on the family. In many cases the mother drops the kids off at the day care center and doesn't see them again for over 12 hours.

Idealism is back, and it's badly needed since it functions in the service of denial. Just look at the worldwide impact of Earth Day 1990. The need to romanticize Mother Earth or the Cosmic Oneness usually conceals problems with our parenting. I once treated a patient who successfully wrote poems about love and was paid well to read them to swooning audiences. The focus of our private sessions for years was on his chronic depression, sexual promiscuity, and his life long inability to love a woman except his mother. I've said it before and I'll say it again: People who overidealize, especially those who do so in public, usually turn out to have grave problems in their private lives. Some people develop addictions, others enter into destructive relationships (Remember, all addictions involve destructive relationships and vice versa). But these are just symptoms. The fundamental problem is a developmental problem resulting in a personality disorder.

LUMPED TOGETHER

Many people try to disguise their problems by joining a group. Sure, there's safety in numbers, but there's also camouflage. Young people are particularly susceptible to this attraction. Here's how one observer put it: "The young today love the group, stripped of all personal effort, for its own sake, and care little where it leads them... The real objective is the ecstasy of freedom from the self, from thought, and especially from morality and of reason; and, of course, from *fear* also."

Recently I treated a patient named Amy, whose life story demonstrates the appeal of group psychology for people who can't find happiness in their individual lives.

Amy met Phil during the anti-war protests of the late '60s. When they were first dating, they went on a lot of marches together and went to all the rallies. Gradually their love for each other became more important than the protest movement. They found themselves wanting to spend quiet time alone together, not screaming slogans and waving signs. They still went to the rallies, but they usually cut out before the event was over. In a short time they started skipping the rallies altogether.

Within a year they married. They had two children, and for a while they were happy with their small circle of friends. But then, for various reasons, the marriage started collapsing.

The first thing both of them did was look for new clubs to join. By the time the divorce was finalized, Amy was vice-president of the local chapter of the National Organization of Women while Phil served as treasurer of the local Zionist organization. As a matter of fact, that's where he met most of the women he began dating.

Dr. Otto F. Kernberg summarized the story of Amy and Phil better than I can: "By asserting its independence of the group, the couple establishes its identity. Dissolution back into the group represents the final haven of freedom for the survivors of a couple that has destroyed itself."

THE MANY AND THE ONE

When two mentally healthy individuals fall in love, they experience fusion and transcendence. They immediately understand, even if only on an intuitive level, the connection between sexuality and spirituality. Through mutual tenderness, they can express their spiritual bond in physical terms.

But by definition, The Group, whatever its structure, perceives physical needs and spirituality to be contradictory and unreconcilable. Think about what you learned in high school history class. Society seems to go through constantly repeating cycles, with repressed puritanical periods at one extreme and periods of unrepressed freedom at the other. Society—the biggest Group of all—is ever competitive with lovers' spiritual and physical union, of which it can never be a part. Thus society incessantly manipulates, controls, "protects," and ultimately attempts to destroy the couple. Think of the couple from pioneer days, in the log cabin, living the pair-bonded life of planting food, raising children, and defending their home with no questions about intention or need for one another. Then comes the town...A general store with seed and necessities ...Then next to it, a tavern...Then next to it, a whorehouse. Our couple's bond becomes more complicated and threatened as the society evolves.

During restrictive periods, group mentality prevails; during more lenient periods, many couples all but self-destruct. As we approach the end of the millennium, we can see the pendulum swinging away from the liberal sixties, with its emphasis on personal freedom, and an era marked by group mentality and idealization. Part of the fallout from that shift is that we have seen many couples self-destruct. That, to me, is why the problem of codependency has cropped up at this moment in history.

As I pointed out in the last chapter, groups such as Alanon offer support to the person suffering from relationship failure and may be extremely valuable in the early phase of recovery—when the seriousness of the problem needs validation. What they *don't* offer is the very thing such a person will soon need: a means of intense close personal introspection. In this regard, self-help groups potentially perpetuate a harmful myth that all human suffering is attributable to external events and situations. Such a philosophy ignores human aggression, dependency needs, and the hunger for love. The members of the group hold out to themselves the false promise of redemption and reconciliation between humans and their psyches, exactly as they did in their previous relationships.

In the words of Wendy Kaminer: "Everybody wants to be reborn, and in recovery [from codependency], everybody is [reborn...because] the divine child inside you is always untouched by the worst of your sins." Self-help meetings aren't the only place people can flee to escape themselves. Under the right circumstances, virtually any group—a church, a political organization, even the Rotary—can provide people with an attractive (but dangerous) alternative to assuming responsibility for their own actions in their private lives.

Groups function by promulgating their ideology through a promise of cohesiveness and the importance of shared beliefs. But my viewpoint as a psychiatrist is diametrically opposed to the ideological one. Psychological insight is healthier than relying on group ideology because it strips away the paranoid delusion that our problems are caused by external events. Insight forces us to confront ourselves and our place in reality—while group mentality simulates the longed for *sameness of* thought, which mother and infant shared in the infant's fantasy, and ignores the reality of father's existence.

Insight also forces us to give up many of our dreams. On the surface that sounds horribly sad. After all, for generations now everyone from Walt Disney to Rodgers and Hammerstein have been telling us to wish upon stars and follow our dreams. But giving up unrealistic dreams and ideals is only one step in the healing process. Once we surrender our fantasies, the next step is to develop the ability to mourn their loss and then move forward with our lives. In doing so we can find new dreams, mature ones that are firmly rooted in reality. For example, we can reconcile our desire to create a better world with a healthy awareness that wars will not end tomorrow.

In my view, the mature human being is one who is relatively free of social constraints, is mature enough to tolerate ambivalence, and is comfortable with the need for both dependency and aggression. Such a person is truly liberated, as he realizes that being independent is an absurdity.

A FEMINIST PERSPECTIVE?

Early on in the history of their movement, feminists identified several problems that needed to be addressed concerning the role of women in society. In a nutshell, these problems were: woman's lack of self-esteem, her dependency on her husband, her role as caretaker, and her continual attempts to please others. If this list sounds familiar, it should. It is virtually a textbook description of the symptoms of codependency.

According to many feminist theorists, women who have not yet been liberated find themselves blamed for the crimes of men. Because they have not been enlightened, they willingly go along with their mate's behavior or addiction, whatever form it may take. But once exposed to the feminist credo, such women come to see themselves as "oppressed." They portray themselves as victims of male chauvinism and trapped by circumstances, but they now realize they must seize the tools of power to overcome their oppression.

Feminism has its good points and its worthwhile goals. Equal wages for equal work and the opportunity for women to hold better jobs will stand as some of the most important accomplishments of twentieth-century society. But I see the same type of danger in this ideology as I see in virtually any other rigid political doctrine. Feminism, in my view, oversimplifies the problem by identifying a convenient "outside force" as the source of all women's ills. Women are victims; if only those controlling men would quit exploiting them, everything would be fine. But as Denise Martin points out: "To reduce dependency issues to alcohol-related behavior blurs the particular role women and men play in society, and it may obscure the fundamental problems within a relationship." In other words, feminist ideology overlooks the role that the mismatching of immature personalities plays in creating unhappy relationships.

It's one thing to want equality in the workplace; it's another thing entirely to deny that differences between the sexes exist. Writing in *Time* magazine recently, Claudia Wallis observes that "Many mid-career women blame the [feminist] movement for not knowing and for emphasizing the wrong issues." All of a sudden, according to Wallis' survey, women who put their careers first find themselves forty years old and childless. She quotes one forty-two-year-old woman as saying: "Our generation was the human sacrifice...We believed the rhetoric. We could control our biological destiny. For a lot of us the clock ran out, and we discovered we couldn't control infertility."

Today, many women are moving away from fundamental feminism; they are searching for ways to unite careers with fulfilling home life. Because the early feminist philosophy overlooked such basic human drives, the movement has had to adapt in order to remain viable. "In the second stage [of the movement]," says Ann Lewis, a founder of the National Women's Political Caucus, "we will not enter the work force as imitators of men. We will not deny the fact that we have children and, yes, think about them during the day. Nor will we deny that we as society's caretakers have responsibility for elderly parents. We bring those values with us." To that I say, Amen—or, even better, "Ah—women!"

Denying the difference between the sexes is the same thing, in psychoanalytic terms, as denying the goodness of the genitals. Hidden in the rhetoric of many social ideals, especially traditional feminism, is this denial; think about it...if both the male and female partner, valued the differences in the sexes and viewed both their own and the other's genitals as good and desirable, they wouldn't need the ideology in the first place. We saw earlier that such denial usually leads to a perversion. And there can be no doubt that perverted sexuality has been on the increase in both men and women over the past two decades. But perversions whether male or female, go to any extreme to hide two basic individual problems: (1) the inability to maintain love; and (2) the amount of underlying hostility.

LOOKING AHEAD

Let me confess to you a fear that I have. I see our society as becoming more and more narcissistic. Virtually everyone in the country is nursing some kind of early developmental wound. Because they don't realize that they seek a magic solution by way of marriage and having children. But since these Neo-parents suffer from a fundamental disorder, their children will surely suffer from early traumas that will affect their own development. And the cycle will repeat again and again....

The Neo-parents: those having children within a trial marriage; those who expect others to raise their children as they pursue income and career; those who believe that sexual adventure proves commitment. Neo-parents all, for they are indeed a *new* version of family and child rearing. As the Old Testament proclaims, God redeemed Israel "for the sake of the children." Without proper intervention and change, the problems for codependency will be passed to yet another generation. The thought of such a Tomorrow is indeed frightening.

I'm not saying there aren't cases where it's better for a child to be raised by one parent, seeing the other only on weekends and receiving birthday cards that tell them "you make weekends special," if the alternative is living in a home where the parents fight continually and are constantly miserable. Nor am I saying that no mothers should work, or that all daycare situations are bad. Many children can receive the support and encouragement they need to develop personalities, capable of lasting relationships if not from the parents, then from the extended family and the stability of a good, safe environment.

If the working mother is still wrestling with her own internal mother, if she resents the fact that she's got a female child, if she is angry because the father is off building his career while she is trapped at home—then the child is not going to feel loved enough. He or she is not going to achieve separation successfully, so problems with dependency and aggression are going to resurface in yet another destructive marriage. And I, or some other physician, will have yet another patient who complains of an inability to maintain a satisfying relationship. To echo the words I've heard, in one form or another, from just about every patient I've talked to in the past few years: "I'm tired, I'm miserable, I'm frightened. This can't go on any longer!"

But for a child who gets enough love, regardless of the source, the possibilities are endless. Love provides the freedom to channel aggression in positive directions. Love neutralizes destructive tendencies in people of all ages. The codependent readily acknowledges their need for love, claiming they didn't get enough, but always minimizing their very own private hate and hostility, which must be accepted before reparation can begin.

As I've explained in this book, our personalities are formed by the events of early childhood, which are colored by the type and degree of nurturance our parents provide, as well as by our inherited strengths and weaknesses. But even people who emerge from adolescence with a fully developed sense of themselves must still contend with the pressure of social and cultural values. Ideally, these values continue nourishing our individuality and our creative endeavors; at worst, they do nothing more than tempt us to regress and run with the pack. Yes, concepts of parenting must change, but so too must our overall sense of cultural values.

Remember, our current social, economic, and political systems are not imposed on us from outside, like orders received from alien beings from outer space. We humans invent such systems and remake them continually according to our own image.

The greatest contribution of psychoanalysis in the past decade is that it has made us aware that we can no longer claim to be the "victims" of these systems. They are creatures of our own devising. If we made them, we can make others that work even better. Professionally, one of the most rewarding moments occurs each time one of my patients realizes that "Marriage problems and a bad marriage haven't happened *to me*. I have simply projected my inner self onto another."

Sources

Beattie, Melody, "The Eighties and Me: Writers Reflect on How Their Books Helped Shape a Decade—and Vice Versa," *Publishers Weekly*, January 5, 1990, p. 22.

———, *Beyond Codependency*. San Francisco: Harper/Hazelton, 1989.

———, *Codependent No More*. San Francisco: Harper/Hazelton, 1987.

Broembsen, F. Von, "Role Identity in Personality Disorders: Validation, Valuation, and Agency in Identity Formation," *American Journal of Psychoanalysis*, 49:2, 1989, pp. 115–25.

Chasseguet-Smirgel, J., In: *Sexuality and Mind*, New York: NY University Press, 1986.

———, "A Metapsychological Study of Perversions." In: *Creativity and Perversion*, New York: W.W. Norton & Co., 1984, pp. 146–61.

———, and Grunberger, Bela, "Epilogue: The Murder of Reality." In: *Freud or Reich?*, New Haven, Conn., Yale University Press, 1986, pp. 218–31.

———, and Grunberger, Bela, "The Internal Contradictions of Freudo-Marxism." In: *Freud or Reich?*, New Haven, Conn.: Yale University Press, 1986, pp 198–217.

———, In: *The Ego Ideal*, trans. by Paul Barrows, New York: W.W. Norton & Co., 1985.

Clower, Virginia L., "Significance of Masturbation in Female Sexual Development and Function," In: Masturbations (from Infancy to Senescence), New York, International University Press, Inc., 1975, pp. 107–43.

Francis, John J., and Marcus, Irwin M., "Masturbation: A Developmental View," In: Masturbations (from Infancy to Senescence), New York, International University Press, Inc., 1975, pp. 9–43.

Goff, J. Larry, and Patricia J., "Trapped In Co-Dependency," *Personnel Journal*, December 1988, pp. 50–57.

Gould, Mark A., *A Consumer's Guide to Psychiatric Diagnosis*. Summit, N.J.: The PIA Press, 1989.

Hall, Calvin S., *A Primer of Freudian Psychology*. New York: New American Library, 1979.

Haynal, Andre, *Depression & Creativity*. New York: International Univ. Press, 1976.

Hershey, David W., "On a Type of Heterosexuality and the Fluidity of Object Relations," presented at Annual Meeting of the American Psychoanalytic Association, Washington, D.C., May 10, 1986.

Jacobson, Edith, *The Self and Object World*. New York: International Univ. Press, 1964.

———, *Depression*. New York: International Univ. Press, 1971.

Kaminer, Wendy, "Chances Are You're Codependent Too" *New York Times Book Review*, February 11, 1990.

Kernberg, Otto F., In: *Object-Relations Theory & Clinical Psychoanalysis*. New York: Aranson, 1981.

———, In: *Passionate Attachments*, Ed. Gaylin and Person, New York: The Free Press, 1988.

———, "Clinical Dimensions of Masochism," *Journal of the American Psychoanalytic Association*, 36:4, 1987, pp. 61-79.

Klein, Melanie, "Early Stages of the Oedipus Conflict." In: *Love, Guilt and Reparation and Other Works, 1921–1954*, New York: The Free Press, 1975, pp. 186–98.

———, In: *Love, Guilt and Reparation and Other Works, 1921–1954*, New York: The Free Press, 1975.

———, "Love, Guilt, and Reparation." In: Klein and Riviere, *Love, Hate and Reparation*, New York: W.W. Norton & Co., 1964.

———, *Envy and Gratitude*. London: Hogarth Press, 1975.

Kunen, James S., "The Dark Side of Love," *People*, October 26, 1987, pp. 89–98.

Mahler, Margaret S., Pine, Fred and Bergman, Anni, *The Psychological Birth of the Human Infant*. New York: Basic Books, 1975.

Martin, Denise, "A Review of the Popular Literature of Co-Dependency," *Contemporary Drug Problems* (Federal Legal Publications, Inc.), 1989, pp. 383–97.

Masterson, James F., *The Real Self*, New York: Brunner/Mazel, Inc., 1985.

McDougall, Joyce, "Epilogue: Illusion and Truth." In: *Theaters of the Mind, Ill. of Truth on Psychoanalytic Stage*. New York: Basic Books, 1985.

———, "The Dead Father: On Early Psychic Trauma and Its Relation to Disturbance in Sexual Identity and in Creative

Activity," *International Journal of Psycho-Analysis*, vol. 70, 1989, pp. 205–19.

Monroe, Scott M., and Steiner, Stephen C., "Social Support and Psychopathology: Interrelations with Preexisting Disorder, Stress, and Personality," *Journal of Abnormal Psychology*, 95:1, 1986, pp. 29–39.

Moore, William T., In: *Masturbations* (from Infancy to Senescence), Marcus and Francis, eds., New York: International University Press, Inc., 1975.

Prest, Layne A., and Storm, Cheryl, "The Codependent Relationships of Compulsive Eaters and Drinkers: Drawing Parallels," *American Journal of Family Therapy*, 16:4, 1988, pp. 339–49.

Price, Neil D., *On The Edge: The Love-Hate World of the Borderline Personality*, Summit, N.J.: The PIA Press, 1989.

Reich, James; Noyes, Russell, Jr., and Troughton, Ed, "Dependent Personality Disorder Associated with Phobic Avoidance in Patients with Panic Disorder," *American Journal of Psychiatry*, 144:3, March 1987, pp. 323–26.

Riviere, Joan, "Hate, Greed, and Aggression." In: Klein and Riviere, *Love, Hate and Reparation*, New York: W.W. Norton & Co., 1964.

Roiphe, Herman, and Galenson, Eleanor, *Infantile Origins of Sexual Identity*. New York: International Univ. Press, 1981.

Segal, Hanna, *Introduction to the Work of Melanie Klein*. New York: Basic Books, 1964.

Shengold, Leonard, "Everything: A Poetic Meditation on Freud's Question, 'What Does A Woman Want?'", *International Journal of Psycho-Analysis*, vol. 70, 1989, pp. 419–22.

Solarides, Charles W., ed., *The World of Emotions*. New York: International Univ. Press, 1977.

Stoller, Robert J., *Perversion, The Erotic Form of Hatred*. American Psychiatric Press, 1975.

Straus, Hal, "The Hemophiliacs of Emotion," *American Health*, June 1988, pp. 61–67.

Treatment of Psychiatric Disorders, vol. 3. Washington, D.C.: American Psychiatric Assn., 1989.

Wallis, Claudia, "Onward, Women!", *Time*, December 4, 1989, pp. 80–87.

Woititz, Janet Geringer, *Adult Children of Alcoholics*. Deerfield Beach, Fla.: Health Communications, Inc., 1983.

———, *Healing Your Sexual Self*, Deerfield Beach, Fla.: Health Communications, Inc., 1989.

Index

Facts About Oakwood Hospital

Oakwood Hospital is a 60-bed, free-standing inpatient psychiatric hospital providing care for adults, adolescents and children, including partial hospitalization services for adults & adolescents. Located in Rockford, Illinois, the facility includes an enclosed outdoor recreation area, indoor gymnasium, community dining room, classrooms and both indoor and outdoor initiatives on the "Escape to Reality" experiential therapy course. Resource Crisis Centers located in surrounding counties are staffed by mental health professionals to provide assessments, referrals, follow-up, and community educational programs.

Referrals to Oakwood Hospital and free assessments can be arranged by the patient, family or health professional 24-hours a day, seven days a week. Call 397-5500 in Rockford or 1-800-843-6251.

Specialty treatment tracks include dual diagnosis (psychiatric and substance abuse), spirituality, attention deficit disorder, ACOA, COA, sexual, physical and emotional abuse and a year round school program. AA & NA meetings are held at the hospital.

Oakwood Hospital offers educational programs and workshops for health professionals, educators, business people and community groups. A speakers bureau is available to address groups on a variety of mental health topics.

Oakwood Hospital: Your Community Mental Health Resource

Oakwood Hospital

**YOUR COMMUNITY
MENTAL HEALTH RESOURCE
1•800•THE OAK 1**